Better Homes and Gardens®

301 decorating
projects & ideas

Meredith® Books
Des Moines, Iowa

301 Decorating Projects & Ideas
Editor: Paula Marshall
Contributing Editor: Cathy Long
Art Director: David Jordan
Publishing Copy Chief: Terri Fredrickson
Publishing Operations Manager: Karen Schirm
Edit and Design Production Coordinator: Mary Lee Gavin
Managers, Book Production: Pam Kvitne, Marjorie J. Schenkelberg, Rick von Holdt, Mark Weaver
Contributing Copy Editor: Ro Sila
Contributing Proofreaders: Becky Danley, Dan Degan, Sue Fetters
Indexer: Kathleen Poole
Editorial Assistant: Kaye Chabot

Meredith® Books
Editor in Chief: Linda Raglan Cunningham
Design Director: Matt Strelecki
Managing Editor: Gregory M. Kayko
Executive Editor: Denise L. Caringer

Publisher: James D. Blume
Executive Director, Marketing: Jeffrey Myers
Executive Director, New Business Development: Todd M. Davis
Executive Director, Sales: Ken Zagor
Director, Operations: George A. Susral
Director, Production: Douglas M. Johnston
Business Director: Jim Leonard

Vice President and General Manager: Douglas J. Guendel

Better Homes and Gardens® Magazine
Editor in Chief: Karol DeWulf Nickell

Meredith Publishing Group
President, Publishing Group: Stephen M. Lacy
Vice President-Publishing Director: Bob Mate

Meredith Corporation
Chairman and Chief Executive Officer: William T. Kerr

In Memoriam: E. T. Meredith III (1933–2003)

All of us at Meredith® Books are dedicated to providing you with information and ideas to enhance your home. We welcome your comments and suggestions. Write to us at: Meredith Books, Home Decorating and Design Editorial Department, 1716 Locust St., Des Moines, IA 50309-3023.

If you would like to purchase any of our home decorating and design, cooking, crafts, gardening, or home improvement books, check wherever quality books are sold. Or visit us at: bhgbooks.com

Make your home a reflection of you

My family is all about comfort when it comes to our home decor. Comfort is important, but I like our home to look stylish. I strive for a decor that's a true reflection of me, my family, and the things we love. But, as I look around my home, I often get the feeling it's time for a change. Sometimes it's a big change and sometimes a small one. Finding the ideas and the inspiration to solve this decorating dilemma is another task. This book is the answer.

Using the ideas in this book, you can pull together a whole new look or simply select a project and add it into your own decorating scheme. The more than 301 projects and ideas in this book are based on the vast experience of the editors of *Better Homes and Gardens* publications. Experience you can draw on to help you start your next successful decorating project.

This book holds something for everyone, including:

- **Inspiration for the casual and the experienced do-it-yourselfer**
- **Projects that can be completed in a few hours or a couple of weekends**
- **Styles ranging from modern to Victorian, country to exotic**
- **Projects in all price ranges, starting with a few dollars to several hundred dollars**

The book is organized by room but many projects can be used in any room. There are projects for all types of do-it-yourselfers. Whether you like to paint, build, or repurpose second-hand finds, here's an idea of the projects you'll find:

- Bar stools refurbished from old school chairs, page 75
- Freestanding garden swing, pages 172–175
- Easy-to-build wine rack, page 57
- Custom columns for architectural interest, pages 22–23
- Sheer fabric-lined walls for an exotic look, page 122–123
- Painted floorcloth with scalloped edges, page 119
- Vintage table repurposed into a bathroom vanity, pages 100–101
- Window boxes for off-season decorating, pages 156–159
- Upholstered screen to add a splash of color, pages 10–11
- Fireplace surround created from architectural salvage, pages 18–19

I hope you find—and make—many projects from this book to make your home the most comfortable and stylish.

Cathy Long, Contributing Editor

So, whether you are looking for a dramatic change in style or one or two fresh ideas to brighten up your decor, I hope this book will give you the inspiration and knowledge to make your home a little bit more you. So don't wait another minute. Grab your paint brush, your hammer, your sewing machine, or your circular saw and start on your next project.

projects & ideas

living

301 decorating projects & ideas

areas

Bring new energy to your living room with these inviting projects. Create a work center from an unfinished computer desk. Give your fireplace a facelift. Introduce old-world style with paint and stenciling techniques. Add seafaring accessories to your decor. Color-wash a mantel. Turn flea market finds into decorating treasures. Make accessories from burlap and felt. Upholster a screen or drape a doorway.

69
projects & ideas

Cottage Cozy

1 Bulletin Board Art

Blue and white gingham bulletin boards are used to hang art on each side of the window. Simply wrap your favorite fabric around the edges of a standard bulletin board and attach to the back with staples or tacks.

2 Wicker Storage

Use wicker baskets to replace drawers and serve as storage cubbies. The baskets keep home office supplies like file folders, catalogs, and books out of sight.

3 Slipcovered Chair

White denim is a sturdy, durable choice for covering furniture. This fabric stands up to normal wear and tear, and it's easy to clean. The star appliqué on the chair's slipcover can be removed before the cover is cleaned.

Note: Sew with right sides together and ½-inch seam allowances unless otherwise noted.

Materials

Note: Materials are for a chair with measurements shown in illustrations. You may need different amounts of materials if your chair is larger or smaller.

- 5 yards (54 inches wide) of natural-color brushed denim fabric
- 1 yard (54 inches wide) of contrasting sage-green fabric for piping and star appliqué
- 15 yards of ½-inch-diameter piping cord. (If you don't want to make your own piping, see note at the end of the instructions.)
- Matching threads
- 12×12-inch piece of fusible transweb paper (for star appliqué)

- Remove seat cushion; it will be covered separately.
- See diagram, *below right*, and measure the following parts of the chair you're going to cover: inside back, seat platform, inside arm, outside arm, arm face, boxed shoulder, and back (skirt will be done separately). Allowing 3 to 4 extra inches all around for ease while fitting the slipcover, use a pencil to mark and then cut patterns for each piece out of kraft paper; allow an extra 6 inches for the seams where the inside back meets the seat platform and where the inside arms meet the seat platform.
- Trace patterns onto wrong side of denim with fabric-marking pencil, keeping fabric on the straight grain (not on the bias). Cut fabric; set aside.
- To make star appliqué on brown kraft paper, draw an equilateral triangle with 8-inch sides, point up. Draw another triangle of the same size, with point down, on top of the first, making a six-point star. Cut out pattern.
- Trace star shape onto transweb paper and fuse to wrong side of contrasting fabric with clothes iron according to manufacturer's directions. (See note

at the end of the instructions.) Cut out and fuse to inside back piece of slipcover. Machine satin-stitch around the edge for a secure fit; or, to be able to remove the appliqué before cleaning the slipcover, baste the appliqué to the denim.

- On the chair itself, mark the vertical center of the inside back, seat platform, and back with straight pins or masking tape. On fabric, mark the vertical center of the same pieces with pins.
- Use T-pins to secure fabric pieces, right side against the chair, to the inside back, seat platform, and back, centering the fabric and the parts of the chair marked with tape or pins; smooth from the center out. Pin pieces to each other in this order: inside back, seat platform, inside arms, outside arms, arm faces, boxed shoulder, and back. Pin fabric a little loosely to slip the cover on and off the chair; you'll have several inches of fabric outside the pinned edges.
- When all the pieces are pinned together, carefully slip the cover from the chair. With a fabric-marking pencil, mark the cutting lines ½ inch outside of the pinned lines to allow for seams. Cut along these marked lines. Mark with a fabric pencil where the denim is pinned, removing the pins as you go. Set aside.
- To make piping, cut 1¾-inch-wide strips of contrasting fabric on the bias.

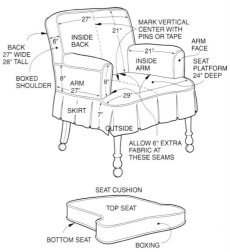

Piece the fabric together as necessary for a 15-yard length. With the right side of the fabric down, lay piping cord in the center of the fabric. Fold fabric to encase cording; pin. Using a zipper foot, machine-stitch fabric as close to the cord as possible.

- To construct the slipcover, work one section at a time. Insert the piping cord into the seams, and, using the zipper foot, stitch pieces together in the same order that you pinned them (inside back, seat platform, inside arms, outside arms, arm faces, boxed shoulder, and back). Trim and clip the seams.
- To make the box-pleated skirt with self-lining, cut denim fabric 15 inches wide, plus ½-inch seam allowances, and as long as the chair's circumference, plus 8 inches for each 2-inch box pleat (the slipcover shown has 16 2-inch-deep box pleats). Stitch the short ends of the skirt together with right sides facing to make a tube.
- Press tube in half lengthwise with wrong sides facing (the wrong sides will be on the outside before you press and facing after you press). Slip cover and skirt into place on the chair. Starting at one corner of the slipcover, make a box pleat. Pin each pleat so the raw edges of the skirt meet the raw edges of the rest of the slipcover. Work around the slipcover. (The cover shown has three pleats evenly spaced on each side and one at each corner.) Remove the cover from the chair. Stitch the skirt to the rest of the

slipcover so the raw edges of the skirt and the slipcover are hidden. Trim and clip the seams.

- Trace the shape of the seat cushion onto kraft paper. Add ½-inch seam allowances on all sides, and cut out one pattern (it works for the top and the bottom).
- Measure the depth and the perimeter of the cushion's boxing. Add ½-inch seam allowances to both measurements; mark, then cut the pattern out of kraft paper. Trace patterns onto denim fabric; cut out, piecing fabric together as necessary for boxing.
- Pin piping to the cushion top; stitch. Pin piping to the cushion bottom and stitch. Pin boxing to piping seam allowance of both the cushion top and the cushion bottom; stitch. Slip cover over the chair.

Note: You can purchase 15 yards of piping at a fabric store instead of making your own. You'll need to buy a 12×12-inch square of fabric for the star appliqué.

4 Upholstered Screen

Divide a room and add a splash of colorful stripes with a folding screen.

- Using a table saw or portable circular saw, sawhorses, and clamps, cut plywood into four panels 12 inches wide and to a height suitable for your home (72 inches is fine for most rooms with standard ceilings). Sand rough edges.
- On a flat, protected surface, use a long-bladed, serrated kitchen knife to cut foam to the same size as the plywood panels (12×72 inches, if you're following this example). Use spray-mount glue to adhere foam to each wood panel.
- Use scissors to cut four rectangles of fleece, wide and long enough so the fleece will stretch around the front side (with foam attached) to the exposed plywood back. Center and stretch fleece over foam, and staple the raw edges to the back side of the plywood. Lay out the striped fabric on panels, arranging the stripes as desired. Cut fabric into four rectangles, each 4

Materials

Note: Fabric and fleece are 54 inches wide.
- 1 sheet of ½-inch plywood, 48x96 inches
- 2 sheets of 1-inch-thick foam (each sheet is 24x72 inches)
- Spray-mount upholstery glue
- 4½ yards of fleece
- 5 yards of striped decorator fabric
- 5 yards of contrasting solid fabric for back
- 20 yards of ½-inch-diameter piping cord
- Matching threads
- 20 yards of 1-inch-wide fusible hem tape
- 6 sets of 30-inch piano hinges with screws (length depends on screen height)

inches longer and wider than plywood (16×76 inches for this example). With fabric-marking pencil, mark a line on the wrong side of the fabric 2 inches in from all outer edges.
- Starting at the center bottom of each fabric panel, place the piping cord just to the inside of the marked line. Fold the fabric allowance (the 2 outside inches) over the cord. With zipper foot, stitch piping into fold, smoothing and pivoting fabric at the corners.
- Center the piped edge of the fabric over the padded wood panel. Smooth and stretch the fabric allowance to the wrong side of the plywood and staple to secure, mitering the extra fabric at the corners. Trim excess fabric.
- Cut four rectangles of solid-color fabric for the back, each 2 inches longer and wider than plywood panels (14×74 inches, for this example). Use fusible hem tape according to the manufacturer's instructions and apply to the raw edge of fabric; with clothes iron, press under 1 inch, mitering corners to remove the excess fabric.
- Use spray-mount glue to adhere solid fabric to the back of the plywood.
- Carefully align the four fabric-covered panels (you'll probably need a helper). With a drill, screw piano hinges so that the two center panels are hinged on the striped-fabric side. Screw the hinges connecting the outer panels to the center section with the hinges on the solid-fabric side; this allows the screen to fold accordion-style and stand freely.

5 Draped Doorway

A white denim curtain with a banded top drapes the doorway between the living room and kitchen. Use a tension rod mounted in the door frame to hang a single pocket-top drape as shown. Add a tieback to hold the drape open.

6 Roman Shade

A pair of Roman shades made from a natural-color fabric provides a stunning contrast against the red walls. The shades are mounted inside the window to show off the painted wood trim. To make, see *Basic Roman Shade, page 88*.

Beautiful Burlap

Burlap is a versatile fabric that offers a great look at a modest price.

1 Pillows

A swatch of expensive fabric, pretty ribbon, and burlap-covered buttons make a burlap pillow as pretty as any traditional-fabric pillow.

- Cut two pieces of burlap to fit a pillow form.
- Place burlap pieces wrong sides together, and machine-stitch three sides. Turn right side out.
- Embellish the pillowcase by sewing on fabric, ribbon, and buttons.
- Slip in the pillow form, and hand-stitch open end to close.

Burlap Basics

Woven from the fibers of the jute plant, burlap was once best known as the material used for making feed bags. Today, manufacturers offer new varieties as additions to decorative lines of fabrics. The advantages of burlap include:

- **Cost:** At $2 to $10 per yard, burlap is the bargain of the material world. Burlap's quality varies with its price. Cheaper burlaps typically offer a loose weave and rough texture, while more costly grades are tightly woven and smoother in appearance and feel.
- **Versatility:** Burlap comes in widths from 36 to 50 inches. Pair it with other materials to add texture and interest to any room. Burlap is also the ideal fabric for embellishments such as buttons, ribbon, braids, cords, tassels, and other goodies from the fabric store.
- **Color:** Burlap is now available in a rainbow of hues, including reds, blues, greens, and pinks. Patterns are also available.
- **Where to shop:** Inquire at your local fabric store to see its selection of burlap.

Beautiful Burlap continued

2 Round Tablecloth

Wider burlap works best for tablecloths.
- Measure the diameter of the table; add to that dimension the distance between the tabletop and the floor. To eliminate a seam down the middle of the tablecloth, plan your cloth so a wide strip of burlap runs down the center, then join the additional burlap to each side of the strip.

- To make a round tablecloth, sew together widths of burlap to create a big square large enough to cover the table and touch the floor. Cut a string so it will stretch half the width of the square. Attach one end of the string to a fabric marker and the other end to a straight pin. Lay the burlap square out flat on a work surface. Push the pin into the center of the cloth. Use your makeshift compass to draw the curve of the tablecloth. Trim along the mark, allowing ½ inch for a hem. Hem the bottom of the tablecloth, or edge the bottom with fringe or fabric as shown.

3 Radiator Cover

Dress up the base of your radiator with a burlap skirt.

- Start with an extra-wide piece of burlap.
- Cut the length of the fabric to 2½ times the width of the radiator. Allow one manufactured edge of the fabric to touch the floor and fold the top edge until the cover-up is the appropriate length.
- Staple the top folded edge of the burlap to the wooden radiator cover, gathering inverted pleats as you go.
- Finish the fabric cover with stapled ribbon along the top edge.

Work with the Drawbacks

Though burlap offers a great look at a modest price, working with it can be somewhat difficult. Here's how to deal with some of the fabric's drawbacks:

- **Protect yourself.** The same fibers that give burlap its pleasing natural texture can float into your eyes and cause irritation, so it's a good idea to wear protective eye gear when cutting or sewing the material.
- **Deodorize.** Some burlap has a slightly unpleasant odor when new. Spray it with a product formulated to eliminate odors from fabrics, such as Febreze.
- **Use discretion.** Even finer weaves of burlap can be a little scratchy, so you probably don't want to use it to cover seating that gets frequent use.
- **Watch for fading.** When using burlap at windows, keep in mind that the colors will fade, but you may not discover it until you take the panels down. Then you'll notice the original color within the folds of the fabric. With burlap costing so little, however, why worry about changing the look of your window treatments a few years down the road?
- **Line the material on most projects;** burlap has a tendency to stretch.

Contemporary Computer Desk

Use unfinished furniture to make an attractive, yet efficient work center.

1 Paint it

Prime the wood and paint the work center the color of your choice. The one shown here is painted green.

2 Chalk it Up

Use chalkboard paint to create a handy spot for jotting notes.

3 Hidden Storage

A canvas curtain, grommets, and steel cables create a hidden storage cubby.
- Sew canvas curtains a few inches wider than desired openings.
- Apply grommets to the curtain tops.
- Hang curtains on steel cables. To suspend cables, screw eyebolts into the hutch frame. Loop cable through the eyebolts and tighten with clamps.

4 Colorful Panel

Add colorful stripes to your home center.
- Cut a panel of ¼-inch plywood to fit the opening between hutch and desk.
- Paint the plywood in stripes of pale yellow, grayed teal, white, orange, lime, and seafoam green.
- Use duct tape to hold panel in place.

5 Drawer Finger Pulls

Use your fingers to open these drawers.
- Remove the old drawer hardware.
- Drill 1-inch holes where the old pulls were attached.
- Sand the holes.

6 Cable Cards

Create an area to hang photos, postcards, and notes. Stretch a piece of wire or cable across the top of the plywood panel. Hold in place with a screw eyebolt, see *Hidden Storage, Project 3*. Use wooden clothespins to hold your favorite photos and cards.

7 Canvas Envelope

Canvas tote bags can be dressed up to fit any decor or purpose.
• Purchase a plain canvas tote bag. Look for canvas envelopes like these at storage specialty and mass-merchandise stores.
• Paint stripes on the envelope to match the hutch opening.
• Add two grommets to the back of the envelope.
• Use coat hooks to hang.
• Store catalogs, blueprints, or papers.

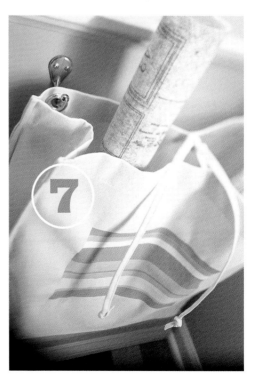

1 Architectural Salvage

If you have a passion for well-worn antiques, extend your passion to your fireplace. This old wood fireplace surround with a well-worn painted finish was found at an antiques store. The mantel is complemented with flanking columns and a mercury-glass mirror above the mantel.

• Take along careful measurements of the firebox and the width and height of the fireplace wall when you shop for a new fireplace surround.

• Tear out the existing fireplace surround. Screw 1×2 nailers into the drywall and studs that will later help hold the new surround in place.

• The center opening of the fireplace surround shown here doesn't snug up to the firebox. Three strips of old tin ceiling panels fill in the gap between the firebox and surround. The old worn paint and embossed design fit in perfectly with the design of the mantel. To give the panels support, wrap them around some pieces of beaded board.

• Pour on buckets of mortar to set the hearth stones in place. Use a trowel to level the mortar before setting the stones. First, attach the beaded board to the hearth's base. Use a rubber mallet to set the stones into the mortar and make them level.

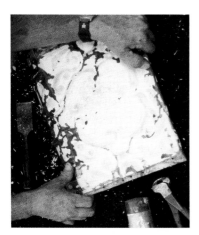

- Position the surround between the existing hearth and the ceiling. Use screws through the sides of the surround and into the nailers to keep it in place. Later, dab matching paint on the screw heads so they blend into the surround.
- For the beaded board that supports the tin, use a table miter saw to cut the pieces neatly, like a picture frame. You can use the table saw to cut the tin as well.
- Use your hands and a rubber mallet to gently bend the tin around the beaded board without flattening out the design, *shown above*. Screw the tin panels into place between the firebox and the surround. Lightly dab the tin panels with green latex paint to make them look as if they've always been a part of the fireplace, but avoid covering up the rust, cracks, and bends. The paint also helps hide the new screws. For an aged look, use a tinted furniture wax in antique brown, such as Briwax.

2 Hearth

Use vintage architectural salvage pieces, found at antiques shops and salvage yards, to visually tie the hearth to the fireplace surround. Look for things like corbels and shelf supports to sit on the mantel. These are interesting to look at because they have so much detail.

3 Lace Valance

An antique lace valance loosely mounted at the window gives an air of simplicity that does not overpower the room.

Select a piece of antique lace that is close to the width of your window. Hang loosely from the top frame and mount using upholsterer's tacks.

4 Ceramic Tile

Layering different tile elements gives this fireplace its distinctive personality. You can avoid extensive labor by covering the existing surround with tile.
- Trowel on a coating of cement mortar and let it cure for a week. This will provide a smooth, solid face to the existing surround.
- Lay the tiles out on the floor arranged in your design.
- Attach the tiles to the fireplace. For the fireplace shown, start with a row of bough-shape tiles across the top of the fireplace, followed by a row of rectangular tiles embossed with pinecones and pine needles.

- Narrower boughs underneath the row create a handsome border effect.
- Brick-shape field tiles follow, providing an unobtrusive background for the large, focal-point panel of two bears.
- Small pinecone tiles trim the firebox.

5 Traditional Moldings

Use a combination of stock moldings to transform a plain wood cover-up into a traditional beauty.

- Work with a cabinetmaker to construct a wood cover-up, like the one shown, for your fireplace. This one is trimmed with a variety of moldings—including fluted pilasters, dentil trim, and a deep crown—for a traditional look. If you like the look of traditional hardwood moldings but want a lightweight material to work with, consider urethane millwork. The products typically won't splinter, crack, or decay, but the pieces can be sawed, nailed, drilled, glued, and painted like wood.

- Add bookshelves to finish out the wall and balance the design.

- Paint the fireplace and shelves in a semigloss white. Roll a rich red paint onto the backs of the shelves and onto the room's remaining walls. The white brightens the room and lends a simple elegance.

6 Arts & Crafts Modern

This fireplace surround with its straight, simple lines is the crowning achievement in this living room.

- The components of this surround are standard pieces available at most lumberyards. The backing is made of tongue-and-groove cedar planks. The mantel is made of medium-density fiberboard (MDF) trimmed with molding. The columns and apron are crafted of 1× pine.
- Take along careful measurements of the firebox and the width and height of the fireplace wall when you shop for materials.
- Assemble the components according to the diagram.
- Prime and paint as suits the decor.

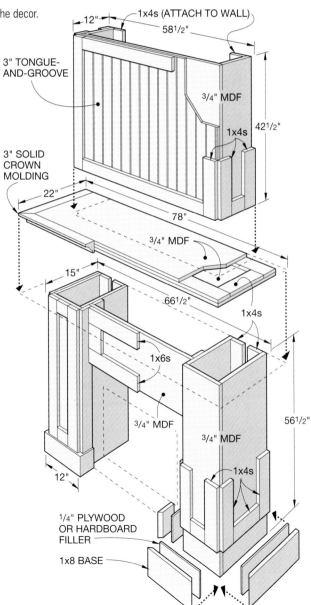

House Dressing

Simple felt projects and custom columns will dress your house in style.

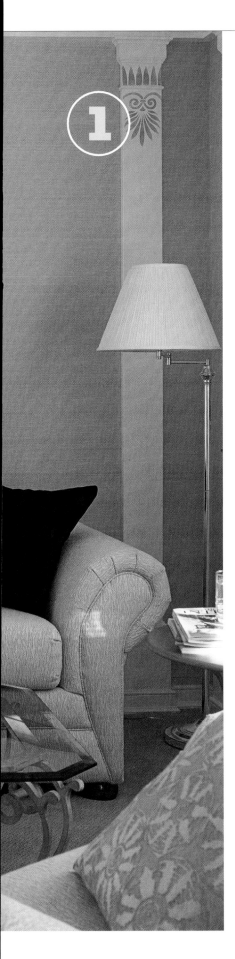

1 Column Conscious

Adding flat columns to living room walls lends architectural interest to a once-plain space.

- Secure a 1×8 board to the wall, making sure it's positioned plumb. If a stud is available, screw through the board and wall material into the stud. Countersink the screw and fill the hole. If no stud is available, use a wall anchor suited to the wall material.
- At the base of the board, use a 12-inch-high 1×10 and finishing nails to box the decorative base as shown. Add a baseboard and cove molding.
- Use a 1×10 and finishing nails to box out the top portion of the column. Add crown molding. Finish with half-round molding as shown.
- Fill holes; let dry. Lightly sand the column. Wipe off residue with a tack cloth. Paint on a primer; let dry. Finish with one or two top coats of color.

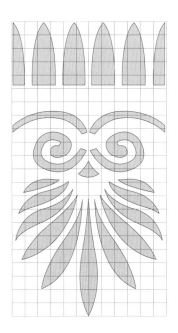

- Once the top coat dries, transfer the stencil design to an acetate sheet and cut out the design with a crafts knife. Use your desired latex or acrylic color and a stencil brush to apply color.

Fashion in Felt

Using felt for no-sew projects offers the advantage of cut edges that won't ravel and don't require hemming. In addition, felt is affordable and comes in a wide range of colors. You can decorate upholstered pieces or pillows quite easily.

2 Woven-Felt Throw

This complicated-looking plaid throw is made by simply weaving together strips of felt.

- Start with three colors of felt in 6-foot lengths (48 inches wide). Cut each color into 48 1-inch-wide strips using a straightedge and a rolling fabric cutter.
- Determine pattern, and lay background strips side by side on a 4×8-foot sheet of plywood laid across a workbench or table. Use masking tape to secure one end of the strips to work surface.
- Fold every other strip back over the tape. Position first perpendicular strip

of felt beside the masking tape and across the felt strips remaining on the work surface.

- Replace folded-back strips on the work surface. Fold back alternate strips and position second perpendicular strip of felt. Replace folded-back strips on work surface, and continue alternating folded-back strips until the throw is completed.
- Remove masking tape. Toward the edges of the throw, iron small squares of fusible tape between felt strips to secure in place.

House Dressing continued

3 Upholstered Bench

You can dress up any plain piece with patterns cut from felt.
- Draw or trace your pattern on paper and cut it out.
- Trace the pattern with a pencil onto felt.
- Cut the pattern out using sharp scissors or a rolling fabric cutter.
- Use crafts glue or iron-on fusible tape to secure the felt pieces to the fabric.

4 Wood Screen

Paint a stunning design onto a new or secondhand wood screen.
- Determine the design for your screen. For a complicated design, it might be helpful to sketch your idea onto paper before starting on the screen itself. For a looser design like the checkerboard on this screen, draw it freehand on the screen panel.
- Prime the screen first to ensure that the paint holds the true color. Your drawn design will still be visible.
- Paint the design onto the panels of the screen. In this checkerboard design, paint all of one color first, let it dry completely, then continue to the next color. This will ensure that your colors won't bleed or smear. Let dry.
- Paint the frame in your color choice.

301 decorating projects & ideas

5 Skirted Table

Trim a table with an easy felt skirting.

- Measure the exposed sides of your table. Here three sides are exposed. Buy felt by the yard that is long enough to make a continuous piece. In this example, two colors of felt create three layers, so three lengths of felt were needed.

- Choose a simple pattern to cut along the edge. Points are easy to make.
- To cut points, use a straightedge and a rolling fabric cutter to make the points around the edges of the felt. The bottom piece is longer and the points are wider. For the top piece, cut two identical strips, then layer the strips, alternating the points.
- Use upholstery tacks to attach directly to the table.

Flea Market Fever

These flea market finds have been refurbished to make five clever and useful projects.

1 Coffee Table Pallet

This rustic coffee table is made from a wooden pallet with deck railing finial legs.
- Purchase a used softwood pallet from a manufacturer or warehouse and four deck finials from your local home center. Each finial comes with a screw embedded in the base.
- Attach the finials to the pallet by first predrilling into the bottom corners of the pallet. Screw the finials into place.
- To instantly age the wood to make the piece look like vintage furniture, you'll need water-base primer, two colors of latex paint, a paintbrush, a candle, and medium-fine sandpaper.

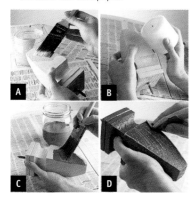

Prime, then let dry. Paint the base coat, *Photo A*; let dry. Rub candle wax on the edges of the wood so the second coat of paint will be easy to remove wherever wax is applied, *Photo B*. Paint the top coat, *Photo C*; let dry. Sand the surfaces to give the paint a weathered look and to partially expose the base-coat color, *Photo D*.
- Use a few beads of clear silicone caulk to secure a tempered-glass top that has been cut to the size of the table.

2 Trunk End Table

Transform an old trunk into an attractive end table with a shelf for inside storage.
- Look for a trunk in somewhat less-than-perfect condition.
- Apply the wall covering of your choice to the inside of the trunk and to the surfaces between wood pieces on the outside. Grass cloth was used on the trunk shown.
- Finials from your local home center can be used for legs.
- Add a plywood shelf to the interior with corner brackets and screws to create inside storage.
- Turn the decorated trunk on end and leave the door open to display books and collections.

3 Armless Dining Chair

Several feed sacks sewn together make a fun slipcover for an armless chair.
- Select an armless dining chair.
- Purchase a variety of feed sacks from a flea market or secondhand shop.
- Measure the chair and cut the feed sacks to show off the labels.
- To achieve the appropriate skirt length, insert a panel of blue ticking and gather it at the back for a slightly imperfect look.
- Add ticking-covered piping for details at the seams.

4 Pillow Roll

A potato sack can make an easy and playful pillow roll.
- Purchase a feed sack and cut out the portion you want to show off, adding seam allowances.
- Stitch fabric edging to sack piece, and sew it into a tube to fit your pillow form.
- Slip the tube over the pillow and tie off the ends with jute twine.

5 Square Pillow

A square pillow can show off an interesting potato sack design.
- Purchase a potato sack and cut out the portion you want to show off, leaving enough for seam allowances.
- Stitch piping into the seams as you sew the two sack pieces together.
- Leave an opening on one side to insert a pillow form. Slip in the form, and hand-stitch to close.

Old feed and potato sacks sell for as little as $5 each at flea markets and farm auctions. Use a fabric-refresher spray to eliminate odors from the sacks.

1 Make a Layer

This loose-fitting half cover protects this upholstered ottoman from stains.

- Select a complementary fabric. Drape the fabric over your ottoman and cut it to the desired size. Cut out a duplicate piece for the lining. Sew the two pieces together.
- Embellish the cap using hand-stitched curtain tiebacks with a tassel on each corner. The piping is part of the tiebacks.
- Add a wooden barrel bead in a neutral color at each corner to dress up the trim.

Dress up your room with one of these stylish ottomans.

2 Refurbish a Footstool

Slipcover a secondhand footstool for a brand new look.

- Purchase an old footstool from a secondhand store. Look for a sturdy stool that is well-proportioned. The footstool shown here lent itself to a skirted box construction, which can be accomplished by first cutting the slipcover top, sides, and overskirt from the same fabric. Sew these pieces together with full welts. The overskirt should hang to within 4 inches of the floor.
- Topstitch the fringed trim to the overskirt. Cut the underskirt from a complementary fabric, and attach it to the overskirt along the seam line, making kick pleats at the corners. The underskirt should skim the floor.
- Slip the cover over the ottoman and tack up the overskirt corners to reveal the underskirt.

3 Construct a Cube

This cube is created using high-density pillow-type foam that is stiff enough to sit on.

- Purchase high-density foam sized to your specifications. The foam can be purchased from a fabric supply store. The cube shown measures 20×20×20 inches.
- Cover the foam block with a fitted fabric cover that has a zipper running around three sides at the top of the cube. The zipper is disguised by a fitted partial topper slipped over the cube.
- Make the topper by draping fabric over the ottoman. Cut the fabric to your desired size. Cut out a duplicate piece of lining and sew the two sections together. Embellish with a lipped welt cord in the seam.

4 Dress a Round Stool

A round stool can be easily dressed up using a purchased pillow with long ties.

- Purchase an unfinished stool from your

local home center. Prime the wood and paint it the color of your choice.
- Top it with a simple tufted pillow with long ties or sew a cushion to fit the stool. To sew the cushion, cut the bottom circle of fabric to the size of the top of the step stool, adding one inch all around for a seam allowance. Cut the top circle two inches larger than the bottom circle. Sew the two pieces together as if making a pillow, catching a gathered ruffle trim and long ties in the seam. These ties wrap around the legs. Stuff pillow with polyester fiberfill. Add a self-covered button at the top for extra detail.

5 Salvage a Drawer

Turn an old dresser drawer into a footstool using basic woodworking skills.

- Purchase an old dresser drawer from a flea market or secondhand shop.
- Prime the drawer and paint it the color of your choice.
- Purchase four legs from an upholstery supply store or home center. Paint them in a complementary color, and then attach.
- Create the top by cutting a piece of ⅜-inch plywood slightly larger than the outside top edges of the drawer and a piece of ¼-inch plywood slightly smaller than the inside of the drawer. Wrap the top of the ⅜-inch piece in foam and cotton batting, stapling them to the underside of the plywood. Cover top with fabric and staple. Cover the ¼-inch plywood with batting and fabric in the same manner. Glue together the back sides of the plywood pieces, using wood glue. Add cord around the edges of the fabric to dress up the finish.
- Line the drawer with a complementary fabric. Adhere the fabric to the drawer with glue.
- Because all drawers are built differently, it's recommended that you reinforce the bottom of the drawer before you sit on the stool.

Old World Style

1 Unfinished Fireplace

This fireplace surround was simply stripped, sanded, and left unfinished. Green marble tops the mantel. Bronze-color paint gives an old fire screen a rich look.

2 High-Speed Stenciling

In creating the living room's stenciled walls, you can use an air-brush painting system that produces a fine spray of color through a handheld nozzle. A motor isn't required to keep paint flowing and it's faster than hand-stenciling. The floral pattern in this living room was inspired by an Islamic floorcloth.

- Paint background walls a neutral color.
- Design and cut one stencil, about 21×36 inches (one-quarter of the repeat). Look for precut stencils at paint stores and home centers.
- Use a second stencil to border the mandorlas (the almond-shape motifs). Add interest by using medallion stencils as part of your design.
- Work your way around the walls in sections. Stencil the lower left quarter of the repeat and flip the stencil over to do the upper left quarter. Water-base acrylics were used in this example.

With fresh paint, stenciling, and artful finishes, this New York apartment reset its style clock with a look that's a bit European and a bit 19th century.

3 Round Tablecloth

The decorative fringe sets off this earthy round tablecloth.

- To make the round tablecloth, start with a textured fabric like a linen or a burlap. Sew together widths of fabric to create a square large enough to cover the table and touch the floor. Cut a string so it will stretch half the width of the square. Attach one end of the string to a fabric marker and the other end to a straight pin. Lay the fabric square out flat on a work surface. Push the pin into the center of the cloth. Use your makeshift compass to draw the curve of the tablecloth. Trim along the mark, allowing ½ inch for a hem. Hem the bottom of the tablecloth, and edge the bottom with a decorative fringe as shown, *right*.

Old World Style continued

4 Customized Shelving

Give a customized look to ordinary shelving units purchased from your local home and garden center.

- Stain the frames of the unpainted shelving unit the color of your choice. These were stained in an ebony color.
- Add decorative upholsterer's tacks for a custom look.

5 Customized Library

Finish three or more of the customized shelving units and place them side by side along a wall for a library-look to showcase books and collectibles.

6 Slipcovered Chair

Slipcovering a chair in a more formal fabric adds to the classic look of the room. This one is similar to the white denim *Slipcovered Chair, page 9.* You'll need a little extra fabric so the slipcover hangs all the way to the floor. If you choose a print fabric with plenty of visual interest, the piping and appliqué are unnecessary. Another way to simplify a

slipcover is to pleat only the corners for fit rather than adding pleats for flair, as on the white denim slipcover on page 8.

7 Stenciled Floor

Enhance your floor by adding a border. Refinish the floor. Before sealing it, add a border between the existing stripes. The overlapping squares shown were stenciled in polyurethane with a dab of raw umber pigment.

- Start at the top of the section you just painted and pull the wood-graining tool down the wall, exerting pressure with your index finger and rocking the tool from top to bottom in one continuous motion. The tool will form a varied series of long, concentric ovals. Use the previously grained strip as a guide by lining up the edge of the tool with the section just painted. Stagger the pattern so that it does not appear too uniform. Wipe excess paint from the tool after each pass.
- Repeat the process, working in 2- to 3-foot sections, until the wall is finished.

Painting Tip:
Stretch the top coat by mixing the paint with glaze in a 4 parts glaze to 1 part paint ratio.

8 Wood-Grained Walls

Any wall can have the rich look of wood with a paint finish called "faux bois" (false wood). If you like the look, here is a simple technique. A wood-graining tool, *above right*, creates elongated oval shapes. Practice this on a primed board before you try it on the wall. You can use any color of paint to achieve this effect, like the purple shown, *center right*. For a rustic, wood-paneled effect, use tan and walnut colors, *below right*.
- Apply base coat to the surface; let dry.
- Brush or roll the top coat paint onto a 2- to 3-foot vertical section of the wall.

Old World Style

9 Raw Talent

If your budget doesn't permit you to purchase new pieces, you can customize affordable unpainted pine pieces with original paint treatments like the armoire in this sitting room which came to life with a leafy stencil and a palette of translucent stains that allows the wood grain to show through.

- To prepare the raw piece, seal it with a water-base polyurethane.
- To get hard edges for each stain color, tape off adjacent sections, something that was especially important in creating the umbra, or shadow effect, on the front and side panels.
- Sponge a coat of golden-oak stain over the panels, then add two more coats on the outer edges of each panel for deeper color and shadow.
- Tape off the outer edges and stencil the leafy motif down the center of each panel in three shades of green, from dark to light. Stenciling was done in latex paint.
- The armoire's crown molding has a brushed-on walnut stain, the panel frames have a sponged-on green stain, and corner details on the sides are a combination of the stain colors.

10 Faux-Bois Walls

The three-step faux-bois paint finish is a challenging technique, so you'll want to practice on old furniture or sample boards before trying a wall. To achieve a realistic effect, study wood grains and experiment with various brushes—art brushes, such as watercolor mops and foam and bristle paintbrushes—even makeup brushes. Every brush and the way you move it will give you a different result, see *Photo A*.

- Over sanded paneling, use a regular paintbrush to apply a coat of oil-base satin-finish paint in an orange-yellow hue, then let it dry.
- For the graining medium, add the following pigments to ½ gallon of clear oil-base glaze:
  2 tablespoons of raw sienna,
  1 tablespoon of burnt sienna,
  1 tablespoon of burnt umber.
  Add a paint conditioner, such as Penetrol®, to keep the paint from getting tacky too fast.
- Divide each panel into quarters. Work on two opposite quarters at a time, taping off the other two as shown, *Photo B*. Use a foam brush and paint two quarters in one direction and the other two in another direction. Pull the brush straight down and twist it down on the left side and then twist it down on the right side, letting up off the surface at the same time to deposit paint in various ways.
- Mimic satinwood over the paneling, beams, and crown molding, giving small moldings and curves

an extra coat or two to keep color value consistent. For a darker hue, add raw umber to the glaze.

- This faux-bois paneling was finished with a coat of polyurethane tinted with raw umber, see *Photo C*.

- Be careful not to mix more than 1 tablespoon of artist's oil with the polyurethane or the mixture will be too opaque.

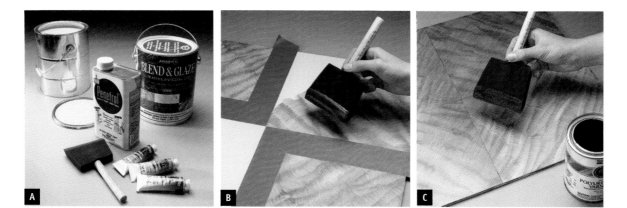

Seafaring Cottage

1 Wallpaper Art

Old wallpaper is hung sideways above the fireplace mantel as a backdrop for an oval mirror. The mirror keeps the wallpaper in place. The curling edges give depth.

2 Seascape

A vintage glass box can show off small treasures and collectibles. The box in this photo holds sand and seashells collected in Florida. A mirror is hung behind the box to bounce light around the small room.

3 Color-Washed Mantel

This mantel has been color-washed in blue to establish an ocean palette for the room.

- Apply a base coat using white satin acrylic latex paint. Allow the base coat to dry for a minimum of 24 hours before applying the wash.
- Mix the glaze in at least a ratio of 4 parts glaze to 1 part light blue paint. Dip a large sponge into the glaze and wring it out just until it stops dripping.
- Dab on the glaze with the wet sponge. Vary the pattern and thickness of the application to emulate the aged look.
- Blend the glaze with a dry brush. After finishing a section, glaze and brush the next section, blending the wet edges. Periodically clean the brush in water.

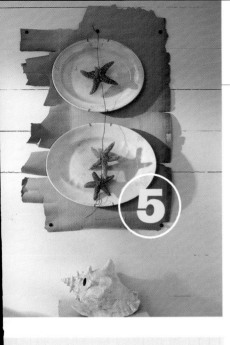

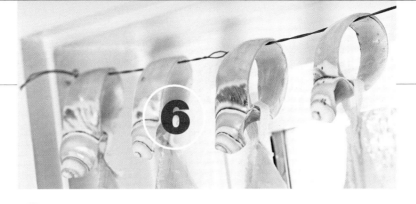

4 Shelf Backdrop

A variety of maps line the back of a white-painted cupboard with open shelving. The shelves square off the back corners of the maps to keep the edges from curling. The maps provide a backdrop to display a collection of dishes and old fans.

5 Plate Appeal

A torn piece of brown paper tacked to the wall makes an easy and inexpensive work of art when teamed with white ironstone plates and starfish.
- Tack or screw a torn piece of brown paper to the wall.
- Using plate hangers, hang two ironstone plates in front of the paper.
- Wind wire around two or three starfish at proper intervals to hang in front of the plates.
- Hang wire from a tack secured to the wall above the plates.

6 Window Hardware

Rather than use a traditional curtain rod, wire is strung to hold this window treatment. Seashell napkin rings hold the curtain in place. Other types of napkin rings will work just as well as long as there is an opening in the ring to hold the window treatment in place, or you may thread a small piece of elastic through the napkin ring and secure it to the curtain using needle and thread on each side of the ring.

7 Window Treatment

An antique lace tablecloth loosely mounted in the window allows plenty of light to shine through even when pulled

shut. Fold the tablecloth over at the top so approximately 8 to 10 inches hang over the edge. Gather sections of the cloth at the fold and hang loosely from the top of the window using shower curtain rings. Thread the rings through a mounted curtain rod.

8 Sun Catchers

Glass bottles can be randomly strung on wire to hang inside a window where they can catch the sunlight. Select bottles of varying sizes and shapes. Wind wire around the neck of the bottle and secure on the window frame using nails. Place additional bottles on the windowsill.

9 Mismatched Art

An empty frame that doesn't match the size of the map behind it creates fun art.
- Use tacks or sticky tack to hang the map, in this case horizontally.
- Attach two eyelet screws approximately one-third of the way down on each side of the frame's back. Center the frame vertically over the map. Secure desired length of picture-hanging wire from each eyelet.
- Mount screws or picture hanger in the wall above the frame.

10 Wire Works

An old wire carrier found at a flea market or antiques shop can be used to hold maps that are rolled up and tied with string. You can also roll up magazines or display a collection of old postcards.

11 Garland of Seashells

Drape a collection of seashells across a basket of magazines. Gather a collection of seashells. Poke a small hole into each shell at the top and the bottom. String fishing line through the shells to create the garland. Use shells of varying shapes and sizes to make a more interesting display.

12 Small Shelf

A balustrade, like the one shown, can be used as a small shelf to hold interesting artifacts, as in this case a starfish. You can find pieces of architectural salvage at flea markets or salvage yards. If you don't find one in the color you are looking for, simply sand the piece, apply one coat of primer, and paint it the color of your choice. If you would like to add a distressed finish, simply follow the instructions for the *Salvaged Mantel, Project 17.*

13 Old Hay Feeder

An old hay feeder that you might find at an antiques shop or farm auction can be mounted on the wall with screws. The hay feeder is the perfect shape to hold books or magazines.

14 Suspended Mirrors

Hand mirrors can be suspended from old chains to add interest to a corner. Purchase old chains with small links from a flea market or buy new chains from your local home center. Attach screw-in hooks to the wall to hold the chains. Various lengths of fishing line are attached to the chains to vary the lengths of the mirrors. A small print or postcard can sit comfortably inside the hooks to add visual appeal above the mirrors.

15 Plate Rack

A hanging plate rack can easily be dressed up by gluing shells of all shapes and sizes or other small accessories to create a pattern of your choice.

16 Map Art

Tack a map to the wall to take the place of artwork. The one shown provides a conversation piece behind the kitchen sink. If you laminate the map, you won't need to worry about the effects of humidity.

17 Salvaged Mantel

A salvaged fireplace mantel that's been distressed makes a nice long shelf with just enough depth to display artwork.
- Brush a coat of paint onto the mantel.
- Put a combination of old and new keys on a large key ring to help vary the texture. Randomly bounce them against the surface to simulate wear.
- Make a few scratches with a coin or a nail; scrape off some paint by dragging the edge of a knife across a few spots.
- Sand through to the wood in random spots, especially edges and corners.

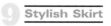

18 Postcard Art

Place laminated postcards along the backsplash behind the sink so you can admire them while washing the dishes.

19 Stylish Skirt

The skirt of a child's dress makes a good cover for an open kitchen shelf.
- Measure the width of the shelf you would like to cover. Allow enough fabric for gathering. Cut the skirt according to your measurements. Hem the sides of the skirt for a finished look.
- Measure the height. If the skirt is too long, you may need to hem to the correct size.
- Mount the skirt to the edge of the shelf using hook-and-loop tape.

20 Postcard Stand

A rusted metal stand that once held food orders at a diner is retooled to display old postcards and black-and-white photos.

21 Wire Artwork

You can hang all kinds of fun things on your wall using wire.
- Make a grid using wire and tiny brass nails. Stretch the wire horizontally between the nails to cover the desired width of wall.
- Hang lengths of wire vertically from horizontal wire at irregular intervals.
- Wrap the vertical wires around the shells or poke a tiny hole to thread the wire through the shells.
- Pin postcards to various spots on the vertical wire.

22 Seaside Tablecloth

Gather the corners of a lacy tablecloth and hang corks, sinkers, and shells using thread or nylon fishing line. Carefully poke a hole in the shell to thread the fishing line through. This easy accent will also work on a side table or as curtain tiebacks.

This one-bedroom retreat shows off clever projects and ideas that evoke memories of the seacoast.

kitch
+dining

301 decorating projects & ideas

ens
rooms

Change the look of your kitchen and dining room with projects for all budgets and styles. Personalize kitchen cabinets with paint or vintage photographs. Build a table using birch plywood and galvanized pipes. Add a shelf to display collections. Divide rooms with a floating wall. Introduce fun window treatments and slipcovers. Add a wine rack or rolling drawer. Create photo art. Make a bar stool.

86 projects & ideas

Vintage Tablecloth Inspiration

A floral patterned tablecloth from the 1940s inspires this cheerful cottage look.

1 Painted Cabinet

The tablecloth used for the window treatments is the inspiration for this cabinet. The recessed panels offer natural divisions for color and pattern.

- Sand and prime an unfinished cabinet. Using latex paint colors that match the tablecloth, brush on base coats of color and let dry.
- To decorate the door and drawer fronts, paint on motifs pulled from the tablecloth, such as flowers or fruit. There are several ways to do this. Paint the design freehand. Draw the design onto tracing paper and transfer it to the cabinet surface. Trace the design onto clear acetate and cut out a stencil with a crafts knife; enlarge the template, *below*, on a copier and use it as a pattern.
- To paint straight lines, such as the checked design on the cabinet's sides, use masking tape to edge the lines.
- Once dry, remove tape, and protect the finish with clear polyurethane.

1 SQUARE = 1 INCH

2 Tablecloth Curtains

A tablecloth with a border pattern is a natural for making a small-size window treatment.

Valance:
- Hem the white band section, or use the finished edge of the tablecloth. Cut a 1× board to the width of the window and screw it to the window trim.
- Attach hook-and-loop tape to the valance and board.
- Mount the valance to the board, gathering it at the corners as shown and staple into the fold, using the fabric to hide the staples.

Cafe Curtains:
- Cut the tablecloth into two cafe-length panels and a valance, allowing ½ inch for hems along cut edges. (The lengths of the panels and valance will depend on your window and the size of the tablecloth.)
- Hem the cut edge on each panel and stitch curtain rings across the top of each; thread swing-arm rods through the rings.

3 Gingham Sheer

This new yellow checked fabric complements the sunny yellow in the vintage tablecloth.
- Cut two shorter panels from the complementary fabric. Stitch a pocket at the panels' top and bottom edges; hem the sides.
- Thread one tension rod through the top pockets and one through the bottom pockets and position the rods inside the window frame.

4 Painted Floorcloth

Stencils and masking tape make painting this floorcloth a snap.
- Start with a 4×6-foot piece of preprimed canvas (available at most art supply stores). Use fabric glue to hem the edges.
- Trace designs from the tablecloth, enlarging the tracings as desired using a copy machine. Transfer designs to the canvas.
- Use a straightedge to mark off squares or borders; use masking tape to edge straight lines before painting.
- Brush on the designs with latex paint in colors that match the tablecloth.
- After the paint has dried completely, remove tape, and then protect the floorcloth with several coats of clear polyurethane.

5 Seat Cushion

This gingham cushion coordinates with the fabric in the window treatment. To make, see *Skirted Seat Cushion, page 67*. Omit the directions for the ruffle.

A Kitchen with Character

1 Tin Tiles

Antique tin tiles dress up the back splashes and the base of the peninsula. They not only complement the age of the home, they're a tough, kid-proof material that handles kicks from swinging legs. The tiles cut easily with tin snips and secure into place with adhesive and finishing nails. Cut tin is sharp, so wear sturdy work gloves.

2 Personalize Cabinets

You can personalize cabinets by gluing meaningful black-and-white photos onto the doors. Choose a favorite family photo. Take it to a photo-processing store and have it enlarged to the desired size. Have them apply a matte, washable laminate finish. Cut the photo to fit within the face frame. Attach with a spray adhesive.

3 Cabinet Makeover

Give laminate cabinets an antique look by combining these drag-painted finish and wood veneer techniques.

Dragged Finish:

Materials

- Trisodium phosphate (TSP) cleaner
- Sanding sponge (for wet sanding)
- Latex primer
- Latex paint for base coat (choose a lighter shade than the top coat)
- Clear glazing medium
- Crafts paint for top coat (choose a darker shade than base coat)
- Burnt umber artist's acrylic paint
- Water-base polyurethane

- Mix trisodium phosphate (TSP) cleaner and water according to package directions. Use the mixture and sanding sponge to clean and roughen the laminate. Rinse well; let dry.
- Brush on primer; let dry. Apply base coat of latex paint; let dry.
- Mix 1 pint glazing medium with one small bottle of crafts paint. Add burnt umber artist's acrylic paint to achieve desired depth of color. (Practice the drag-painting technique on scrap wood or poster board before you begin on your project.) Brush glaze mixture over base coat. Work in small sections, so glaze doesn't set prior to dragging.
- Use gentle pressure to drag tool/brush in one direction through glaze. Overlap sections to eliminate visible seams. Let dry. Apply one or two coats of clear water-base polyurethane.

Easy Veneer:

Materials

- Wood veneer (quantity will vary, depending on the number of cabinets you cover)
- Contact cement
- Polyurethane (optional)

- Make sure cabinet surface is clean and dry. Use a pencil, straightedge, and utility knife to measure and cut wood veneer to fit the door panel. (If the door panel is slightly uneven, cut the veneer piece ½ inch larger than the panel all the way around. Once secured to the surface, use the utility knife to trim the edges to fit.) Follow the manufacturer's directions for applying contact cement. With a paintbrush, apply the cement to the cabinet surface as well as to the back of the veneer.
- Once the cement dries, carefully align the veneer and press into place. (Be sure to position the veneer correctly because it is nearly impossible to lift and reposition it.) Use a rubber roller to apply pressure from the center of the veneer to the edges to remove air bubbles. For most veneers, it's a good idea to apply one light coat of polyurethane to protect the surface from moisture and stains.

This kitchen and dining room was redone using a combination of paint finishes, tin tiles, and fun fabric to bring out some of the old-house character.

kitchens + dining rooms

A Kitchen with Character continued

4 Privacy Shutters

Tin tile fronts give these simple shutters period charm.

Materials
- Mahogany (or other wood), ripped to 3 inches wide
- Vintage (or reproduction) tin ceiling tiles
- ⅛-inch mahogany veneer
- Wood glue
- 4d finishing nails
- Off-white latex paint
- Clear water-base polyurethane
- Brads
- Decorative handles
- Hinges
- ½-inch wood screws

- Construct basic frames from mahogany to fit your window. Using a table saw, rip mahogany to desired width, miter corners, and cut a ¼×¼-inch rabbet along each inside edge. Join frame components with wood glue and 4d finishing nails. Clamp overnight.
- In the meantime, use a garden hose and pressure nozzle to dislodge loose paint from tin ceiling tiles. Use tin snips to cut tiles to fit frames. Brush tiles with white latex paint.
- To fill in gaps where paint has chipped off, dab on paint with a rag. When dry, coat with polyurethane; let dry.
- Fit tiles into rabbet on back of mahogany frame.
- Cut mahogany veneer to fit inside rabbet; slip into place.
- Use brads to secure veneer within frame. Screw decorative handles to front of frames. Attach shutters to wall with hinges and wood screws.

5 Crackle-Finish Mantel

This salvaged antique fireplace mantel looks even older with a crackle finish.

Materials
- Mantel or another piece of furniture
- Latex primer
- Latex paint for base coat (a dark color, such as cobalt blue) and top coat (white)
- Crackle medium

- If the surface to be painted is grimy, use a garden hose fitted with a pressure nozzle to wash the dirt off. Lightly sand splinters or very rough spots, but leave some imperfections to add to the antique look. Apply primer with a paintbrush; let dry. Apply the dark base coat; let dry for 24 hours.
- Use paintbrush to apply crackle medium over base coat. Follow manufacturer's instructions for drying time, but you should typically wait at least 1 hour and no more than 4 hours before applying the top coat. When crackle medium is set, brush on white top coat. (Be careful not to drag the brush into another painted area or you'll carry over the crackle medium.) As the paint dries, the finish will crackle before your eyes.

6 Painted Fabric

Paint fabric for slipcovers or window treatments to complement your decor.

Materials
- Heavy white canvas or other upholstery-quality fabric
- Permanent black marking pen
- Fabric paints

- Find a 1940s tablecloth or tea towel for inspiration. Trace or photocopy the motif onto paper. Place carbon paper between the canvas and the paper pattern, and trace over the pattern with a pencil to transfer the design onto the canvas. Outline the traced design on the canvas with a permanent black marking pen.
- Study the tablecloth or tea towel and repeat the colors as shown, or determine your own color palette. Practice on scrap fabric until you get the look you want.
- With an artist's brush, apply fabric paint at the center of the design first, then brush on the color surrounding the center. Follow the paint label's directions for setting the color.

7 Mosaic Tabletop

A pair of old table legs support a plywood countertop covered by a mosaic of broken tiles and ceramic plates.

- Lay out broken pieces of tile and plates around the project's perimeter. Arrange pieces from the outside edges in. To avoid having jagged or rough edges, use tiles that retain the manufacturer's beveled edge.
- Apply mastic to your surface. Position tile pieces on the mastic, leaving ¼- to ½-inch spaces in between; let dry overnight. (If any tiles pop off, reapply using more mastic.)
- Use a spatula or your gloved hand to spread tile grout over the mosaic, pressing grout into the spaces between pieces and gently scraping excess off the top. Wipe off residue from tiles with a damp sponge. Let dry according to manufacturer's directions. When you are sure grout is completely dry, seal with a grout sealer.

Photo Finish

1 Custom Roman Shade

This Roman shade is customized by using
three fabrics on the width of the shade.
To make, measure the window as you
would for a single-fabric shade. For each
vertical seam, add 2 inches to the overall
width of the shade. For example, if your
finished shade will be 48 inches wide,
the full width of all three fabric pieces
before sewing will be 52 inches: 48 plus
1 inch on each side for the pattern, plus
1 inch for each of two lengthwise seams.
First, sew the fabric panels together.
To cover the seams, sew a decorative
trim along the right side of the shade.
Then continue making according to the
instruction for the *Basic Roman Shade,
page 88*.

2 Table Covering

A linen table covering gives an updated
look to a hand-me-down wood table and
four metal chairs. To make a similar table
covering, see the instructions for the
Round Tablecloth, page 31. Instead of
making the table covering floor length,
allow for a 6-inch drop from the edge of
the table and a 2-inch hem.

3 Freestanding Divider

This floating wall was purposely built shorter than the ceiling to make the room seem taller.

Materials

- Two 2×4s, 69 inches long, for the frame stiles (A)
- Two 2×4s, 48 inches long, for the frame rails (B)
- Two 2×4s, 16 inches long, for the window stiles (C)
- Two 2×4s, 45 inches long, for window rails (D)

From three sheets of ¼-inch birch plywood (see *Buying Hardwood, Plywood, and Lumber, below*) cut:

- One frame top skin (E), 3½×48 inches
- Two frame side skins (F), 3½×72¼ inches
- Two window rail skins (G), 3½×36 inches
- Two window stile skins (H), 3½×15½ inches
- Two panels skins (I), 48½×72¼ inches

Other Components:

- No. 8×2½-inch deck screws
- Two 1-inch pipe flanges
- Two 1-inch-diameter galvanized pipes, 40 inches long, threaded on both ends
- Wood glue
- 4d finishing nails
- Two 1-inch galvanized pipe tees
- Four 9-inch lengths 1-inch galvanized pipe
- Four 1-inch galvanized 90-degree pipe elbows
- Wood putty
- Interior acrylic primer
- Paint

- Assemble frame stiles (A) and rails (B) with 2½-inch screws. Position the window stiles (C) between window rails (D) as shown in the diagram, *right*, and attach with screws. Position assembled window frame within the wall frame, and screw it into place.
- Attach two 1-inch pipe flanges to the underside of the lower window rail, centering one under each window stile. Drill two 1⅛-inch-diameter holes in the lower frame rail where shown. Insert the pipes through the holes, and use a pipe wrench to tighten them into the flanges. (These pipes give the wall rigidity.)
- Attach top and side frame skins (E and F) to the frame with glue and 4d finishing nails. Install the window rail skins (G) next, then the window stile skins (H).
- With a measuring tape and pencil, mark the window opening on the panel skins (I), then use a jigsaw to cut about ¼ inch inside the lines. Apply a thin bead of wood glue to one side of the frame assembly, position one panel skin squarely on the frame, and nail the skin to the frame. Flip the frame over, and attach the other skin in the same way.
- Using a router with a flush-trim bit, trim the skin panels flush with the surface of the window frame skins. Carefully square-up the corners with a handsaw.

- Use a pipe wrench to assemble the pipe feet from tees, 1-inch pipe, and elbows, as in the diagram, *below*, then thread them onto the pipe extending from the lower frame rail.
- Fill any nail holes with putty, sand surfaces smooth, and paint the divider wall with one coat of acrylic primer and two coats of paint, letting the paint dry between coats.

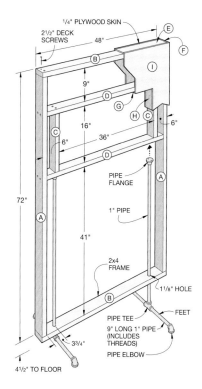

Buying Hardwood, Plywood, and Lumber

Most home centers carry limited species of hardwood plywood and lumber, usually only oak and birch. To find the cherry plywood and lumber used in this project, go to a store that specializes in hardwood lumber.

Hardwood plywood has a thin veneer of hardwood over a laminated core, which looks like regular plywood, or a medium-density fiberboard (MDF) core. Either type will work for this project, although MDF-core plywood is somewhat heavier and produces fine dust when cut. Use a dust-collection system when cutting MDF-core plywood.

Hardwood lumber is sized differently than regular softwood dimensional lumber, based on its rough-cut thickness prior to milling or surfacing. Lumber cut 4/4, or four-quarter, is initially cut 1 inch thick, and 8/4 (eight-quarter) lumber starts out 2 inches thick. Most hardwood retailers will mill lumber to the sizes you need for an additional charge.

Family photographs that replace artwork are the focal point of this dining room.

Photo Art

Add a personal touch to your wall by enlarging family photographs.

- Take the photos you would like to hang to a copy store and have them enlarged and transferred to white canvas. If the photos are different sizes, center them within the same-size canvases for a unified look. In most cases, copy stores can make these types of canvases up to 3 feet wide and any length.

- Sandwich the top and bottom edges of each canvas panel between pairs of 1×4s cut slightly wider than the canvas and brushed with polyurethane. Screw the boards together.
- To hang, mount the top board's bottom edge on nails driven into the wall.

5 Hanging Shelves

These hanging shelves use no floor space, but provide plenty of display appeal.

Materials

- Four ⅜-inch-diameter threaded rods, 72 inches long
- Four ⅜-inch 16×3-inch hanger bolts
- Twenty-eight ⅜-inch hex nuts
- Twenty-eight ⅜-inch fender washers
- Four ⅜-inch coupling nuts
- Polyurethane
- From one-half sheet (30×60 inches) of 18-millimeter (¾-inch) Baltic birch plywood, cut three 19¾×18-inch shelves.

- Cut a 45-degree bevel on the edges of each shelf so they look like the one shown, see *lower center*.
- Stack the shelves, clamp, and drill ⅜-inch holes for the threaded rods; the holes form a square with 16-inch sides center to center. Sand the shelves smooth and apply two coats of polyurethane.
- Using a stud finder or nail, locate ceiling joists where shelf unit will hang. Drill ⅛-inch pilot holes, and drive hanger bolts into the joists by spinning a nut onto the machine-thread end and turning the nut with a wrench, see Hardware Assembly Detail, *lower right*. Put a fender washer over each hanger bolt, and install coupling nuts.
- Assemble the shelves and rods loosely with fender washers and nuts above and below each shelf, see Exploded View, *upper right*. The rods should turn freely. Position the shelf unit beneath the coupling nuts, and thread each rod into a coupling nut until tight. Adjust each shelf until it is level by raising or lowering the nuts below the shelf, then tightening the nuts with a wrench.

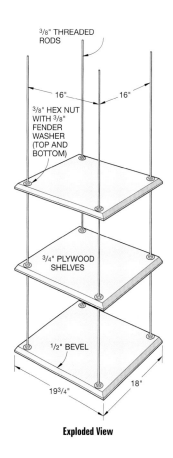

⅜" THREADED RODS

16"   16"

⅜" HEX NUT WITH ⅜" FENDER WASHER (TOP AND BOTTOM)

¾" PLYWOOD SHELVES

½" BEVEL

19¾"   18"

Exploded View

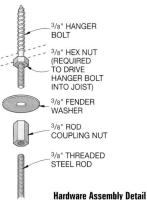

⅜" HANGER BOLT

⅜" HEX NUT (REQUIRED TO DRIVE HANGER BOLT INTO JOIST)

⅜" FENDER WASHER

⅜" ROD COUPLING NUT

⅜" THREADED STEEL ROD

Hardware Assembly Detail

Retro Kitchen

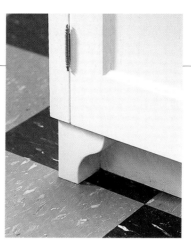

1 Floor Tiles

On the floor, flecked flooring tiles alternated in black and gray enhance the kitchen's vintage style.

2 Cabinet Feet

Tuck these feet into the toe-kicks to instantly create the look of freestanding furniture.

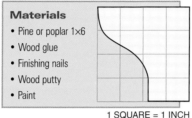

Materials
- Pine or poplar 1×6
- Wood glue
- Finishing nails
- Wood putty
- Paint

1 SQUARE = 1 INCH

- Cut four 4-inch squares from pine or poplar 1× board. Place two squares atop the other two squares. Use wood glue to laminate each stack of blocks, creating blanks. Clamp both blanks; let dry overnight.
- To transfer the cabinet foot pattern, *above*, onto the blanks' surfaces, draw the pattern's 1-inch grid to actual size on heavy paper. Measure your toe-kick to be sure this size foot will fit; adjust if necessary. Draw the pattern as shown, using the grid marks as guidelines. Place carbon paper on the surface of a blank, top with the paper pattern, and trace the outline with a pencil. Repeat tracing step on the second blank.
- Cut out the feet with a band saw or jigsaw. Sand the feet. Secure the feet to the toe-kick with finishing nails. Countersink with a nail set. Fill holes with wood putty, let dry, sand, and paint to finish.

This retro kitchen is loaded with nostalgia, which started with an antique Tappan range for inspiration.

Retro Kitchen

3 Vintage Aprons

Hang vintage aprons on the wall in your kitchen to take the place of artwork.

4 Open Shelving

Leave cabinet doors off and create open shelving to display glassware or collections.

5 Display Shelf

A long shelf mounted above a table is a great place to display collections.

Materials
- Pine or poplar 1×12, 8 feet long for shelf (A)
- Pine or poplar 1×10, 8 feet long, for bottom rail (B)
- Scrap of 2×8 (or wider), 3 feet long, for brackets (C)
- 3-inch crown molding, 10 feet long (D)
- Wood glue
- 4d finishing nails
- 1½-inch screws
- Concealable hanging hardware
- Wood putty
- Paint

- To make brackets (C), cut four 7-inch squares from scrap 2× board. Place two of the squares atop the other two squares. Use wood glue to laminate each pair of stacked blocks, creating blanks. Clamp both blanks, and let dry overnight.
- To transfer the bracket pattern, see Diagram A, *below*, onto the wood, first draw the pattern's 1-inch grid to actual size on heavy paper, duplicating the number of squares shown. Draw the pattern as shown, using the grid marks as guidelines. Then place carbon paper on the surface of a blank, top with the pattern, and trace the outline with a

pencil. Repeat the tracing step on the second blank. Cut out the brackets with a jigsaw. Sand each bracket and set aside.
- To build the shelf, rip the 1×12 to 10 inches wide, then bevel one long edge to 45 degrees to create the shelf top. Reserve the 1½-inch-wide strip removed during rip-cutting to use as spacer between shelf (A) and bottom rail (B).
- From the 1×10, rip a second 1½-inch-wide spacer. Use remaining 7¾-inch-wide board as bottom rail (B). Screw spacers to the bottom rail, and position brackets (C) under it. Screw through bottom rail into the top of each bracket. Glue the shelf to the spacers, making sure to position the shelf's beveled edge at the front and angling down, see Diagram B, *below left*. Countersink screws. Cut two 10-inch lengths of 3-inch crown molding (D) for sides; cut 8-foot length for front. Miter the corners that will meet. Secure the molding to shelf's front and end edges with finishing nails. Countersink the nails; fill holes with wood putty. Let dry; sand. Paint shelf. Use concealable hardware to secure shelf to wall studs.

6 Wine Rack

Take the door off a cabinet, slip in this easy-to-build wine rack, and nail it into place.

Materials
- Pine or poplar 1×4 for front panel (A)
- ¾-inch plywood for bottom rail (B)
- Wood glue
- 4d finishing nails or 1½-inch-long screws
- Wood putty
- Paint

- Measure width of cabinet-box interior. With a circular saw or table saw, rip 1×4 to 2½ inches wide and the same length as the width of cabinet-box interior for front panel (A). For bottom rail (B), cut ¾-inch plywood 10 inches long and the same width as cabinet-box interior. Use a router with ½-inch

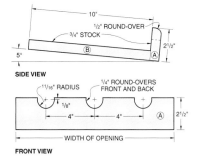

SIDE VIEW

FRONT VIEW

round-over bit to round off the front panel's top front edge. Use a compass or half-dollar-size object to mark the front panel with rounded notches that will hold bottle necks, spacing them about 4 inches apart on center. Cut rounded notches with jigsaw, rounding off the inside of the notches with a router fitted with a ¼-inch round-over bit.
- Glue the wine rack front to the edge of the wine rack bottom; secure with finishing nails. Countersink nails, fill the holes with wood putty, let dry, and sand. Paint as desired. Toenail the rack inside the existing cabinet so it tips slightly forward, see illustration, *above*. Or, if you have access to both outside surfaces of the cabinet, screw through the cabinet sides and into the rack sides to secure. Countersink the screws, fill the holes with wood putty, let dry, sand, and paint to match.

Diagram B

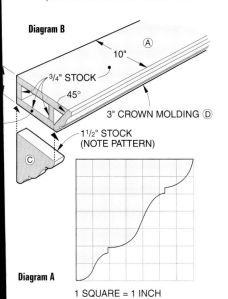

10"
3/4" STOCK
45°
3" CROWN MOLDING (D)
1½" STOCK (NOTE PATTERN)

Diagram A

1 SQUARE = 1 INCH

Sunny Dining Room

1 Window Treatment

Simple sheer curtains edged with a sturdier fabric border are threaded onto a thin steel cable held taut by turnbuckles for a nautical twist.

- Cut sheer fabric twice as wide as the windows (so there's plenty to gather), plus ½-inch seam allowances. If your window is exceptionally wide, plan for two narrower curtains instead of a single wide one. Turn short ends under ½ inch, press with clothes iron, then hem. Cut the contrasting fabric, which is sewn to the top and bottom of the sheers, 5 inches wide (4 inches for the border, plus seam allowances). Piece the border fabric so it's long enough to span the length of the sheer.
- Once the fabric for the curtain and border is cut, pin the border to the sheer so all raw edges are hidden. Sew the border fabric to the top and bottom of the sheer.

- At regular intervals along the top of the curtain (every 4 to 6 inches, depending on the look you want and the width of the window), use a grommet tool to insert grommets. Set the curtain aside and start setting up the window hardware.
- Purchase four screw eyes, two turnbuckles, and thin steel cable at your local home center. The cable should measure twice the height of the window opening, plus its width, and another 1 to 2 inches to thread into the turnbuckles. At the bottom of the window frame near the ends, and along the sides of the frame near the top of the window, drill pilot holes into the window frame or sill, then insert the screw eyes.
- Loop one end of the steel cable into the turnbuckle and tighten to secure. Run the other end of the cable up through the screw eye on the same side of the window at the top, thread it through the grommets on the curtain, then run it through the screw eye on the other side of the window. Insert the end into the second turnbuckle, tighten it to secure, then hook both turnbuckles into the screw eyes on the windowsill. Tighten, if necessary, to increase the tension on the cable to hold the curtain taut.

2 Checkered Floor

A bold checkerboard design was painted over this 1970s-era linoleum, turning the squares on the bias so the pattern makes the room look larger.

- Roll a quality primer over the entire floor and let dry according to the manufacturer's directions. Determine the colors you want on the floor. Roll the lighter hue over the entire floor and let dry.
- Figure out the best size for the checks: Spacious rooms should have larger (12- to 14-inch) squares; modest-size rooms look better with smaller-scale squares (8 to 10 inches). Once you've decided how big the squares will be, measure the room and mark lines with a yardstick and pencil. Tape off the squares that will be painted.
- Dilute concrete stain with mineral spirits in a paint tray until it's of waterlike consistency. Use a small roller for quick, even application, or try a natural-bristle brush for a streaked effect. Allow to dry, then remove tape.
- To add durability, apply one to two coats of clear polyurethane over the floor with a large roller. Let dry between coats.

This dining room's checkerboard floor and sheer window treatments complement the solid yellow walls and bamboo furniture for a fresh, sunny look.

Industrial Strength

This kitchen uses brave color and unconventional materials to achieve a new look.

1 Metal Fronts

These metal door and drawer inserts complement the different metal materials used in this kitchen.

- For the galvanized-metal door and drawer inserts, order cabinetry minus the recessed panels, as if you are going to put glass in them. Carefully measure the openings from the back so that you include the width of the rabbeted groove in your dimensions. Then subtract to allow a 1/16-inch clearance all the way around. Because the galvanized metal is heavy, you'll want to have a metal fabricator cut the panels to size.
- Position each panel within the opening, making sure it fits flat against the rabbeted groove. Apply a bead of caulk all the way around the back perimeter of the panel to secure.
- Leave flat to dry. Install doors and drawer fronts.

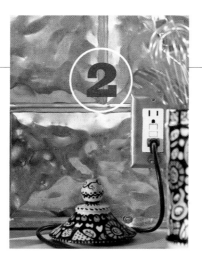

Galvanized Backsplash

Galvanized exterior skirting for manufactured homes is used for this backsplash. The skirting is available from your local home center.

- To prepare a sheet for application on a wall, use a dry erase marking pen to indicate locations of cutouts for electrical outlets and other obstacles. (Remaining marks can be easily wiped off later.) If you're a novice at cutting wall panels, you may want to create a template of the wall area using a piece of poster board or cardboard. Make sure your template fits, then transfer your markings to the metal sheet.
- Use metal shears to cut the sheet. To create openings within the sheet, such as for an outlet, first punch a hole in the proposed opening using a nail. Then, slip the tip of the shears into the nail hole to get started.
- Apply construction adhesive to the section of wall where you plan to position the metal sheet. (Don't position adhesive too close to the edges or it will push out from beneath the sheet when pressed into place.)
- Cut the next metal sheet as needed, position, and apply the sheet using construction adhesive. One sheet should slightly overlap the next. (Determine which sheet to overlap by studying which position makes the seam least visible from prominent entries into the room.)
- Secure seams using button washers and finish nails to create an industrial/riveted look, see *above*. Use a nail set to sink the nails into the center of the washers.
- To bend sheets around corners, position a metal straightedge where you want the sheet to bend, then press and bend the sheet.
- For wainscoting, apply sheets following the same procedure. Use moldings to conceal exposed top and bottom edges.

Refrigerator Skin

Accurate measurements are the secret in creating this refrigerator "skin" from galvanized sheets.

- Use a metal fabricator to cut and shape the galvanized sheets to create the skin. The fabricator must bend the sheets for the sides and doors so they wrap around corners of the refrigerator doors and sides. (Each skin should resemble a metal tray when properly formed.) Keep in mind that it is the inside dimension of the "trays" that must snugly fit over the refrigerator doors and sides.
- The galvanized top for the refrigerator can be cut as a flat sheet and doesn't need bending. Instead, install it first, then install the side trays so the edges hold the top in place and the seams are concealed.
- To install the skin, spray the inside of the metal section with spray adhesive. Then tap the skin onto the side or door using a 2×4 or rubber mallet. Start at opposing corners and gradually work around the door.
- When installing the door sections, the lips of the tray must be deep enough to wrap around to meet the rubber seals on the door. Use metal shears to make the panel fit precisely.
- Handle options include stainless steel and the less expensive alternative, metal piping.

kitchens + dining rooms

Industrial Strength continued

4 Window Treatment

Decorative trim adds a splash of color to this black and white checked window treatment.

- To cut the fabric to size, measure the width for the valance (2 to 4 inches wider than the window), plus two times the depth of the rod (usually 1½ to 3 inches). Add a 1-inch seam allowance. Determine the desired height of the valance. Add 2 inches for the hem and 4 inches for the rod pocket. Cut the fabric to this width and length.
- To make the valance, sew the bottom using a standard hem stitch.
- Then fold under each side of the fabric ½ inch and stitch.
- To make a pocket for the valance rod, fold the top under ½ inch and press. Then fold under another 3½ inches and press. Run a seam ¼ inch from the bottom.
- Sew pom-poms along the bottom edge 1 inch apart.
- Slide the rod into the pocket, and attach the rod to the wall according to the manufacturer's instructions.

301 decorating projects & ideas

5 Table Topper

This tablecloth is placed on the diagonal so the colorful red rickrack stands out. To determine the size of the table topper, measure the length and width of your table and add 2 inches for the hem. Hem the fabric. Hand-stitch jumbo rickrack along the bottom edges of the fabric.

7 Rolling Drawer

Mount a wine box on casters and store it underneath the center island to serve as a "rolling drawer."

6 Concrete Countertops

Concrete countertops provide durable, good-looking work surfaces that complement the metal materials.

- There are two options for installation for concrete countertops. One is to have the countertops cast at another site, then brought to your home and installed. The other is to have the countertops poured in place, as was the case for this kitchen. Pouring concrete countertops isn't a job for anyone inexperienced in working with cement, so first hire a contractor to assist you. Start with an underlayment of CDX ¾-inch plywood topped with cement backer board. Both materials are set into the tops of the cabinets so that the top of the backer board is flush with the top of the base cabinet. Brace boards, typically 2× lumber, go wherever they won't interfere with drawers, such as at stiles. Screw through the cabinet faces and toenail into cabinet backs to secure the braces in place.
- To hold the concrete to shape and height, build a form with lumber and temporarily attach it to the cabinet. In the kitchen shown, the aluminum angle was used as the form, secured to the cabinet tops and backerboard, and left in place as a decorative edging.
- When using a temporary wooden form to shape the concrete countertop, it's a good idea to run an electric palm sander around the perimeter of the form once the concrete has been poured. The vibrations of the sander help the concrete settle against the wood form and create a smoother edge.

- For a smooth countertop, use a 10-sack grade of Portland cement mixed with plenty of sand. After mixing in water, the cement should be the consistency of thick oatmeal.
- Use a float to smooth the surface. Keep floating and misting with water as necessary until a sheen forms.
- For variety, color, insets of metal, or other materials or objects can be added to concrete.
- Use a clear epoxy coating formulated for garage floors to seal the surface and protect it from stains and to hide any cracks that manage to sneak in.

8 Chalkboard Dishwasher

Your kids will always have something to do in the kitchen with this chalkboard dishwasher front.

- Order a custom-cut ⅛-inch-thick chalkboard from your local school supply company. To install, take off the trim on the dishwasher front, then remove the existing decorative panel and cardboard piece underneath.
- Put the chalkboard in place and reattach the trim. If the holes for reattaching the trim don't line up exactly because the chalkboard is thicker than the original decorative panels, drill new holes.

Scandinavian Influence

1 Painted Cabinets

If your cupboards are in good shape, give them a new look using a little elbow grease and paint.

- Clean the surface with a good cleanser, such as trisodium phosphate (TSP) and water. Remove the doors, drawers, and hardware. Lightly sand the existing finish to smooth the surfaces and prepare them for painting. Use a tack cloth to wipe away sanding residue. If your cabinets are covered by many layers of paint, you may have to strip off the old finishes. To make the job go faster, take doors and drawers to a professional for stripping, then use a belt sander or mild stripping solution to remove the paint from the cabinet boxes at home.

- If you want to make a set of upper and lower cabinets look like a hutch, *opposite page*, install beaded board on the walls behind a section of upper shelves. Paint all cabinet frames and interiors with primer, let dry. Paint with two or three coats of high-quality white latex enamel paint. Cabinet doors and drawer fronts that will be part of the "hutch" should be painted white. Paint the remaining doors rich red.

- To complete the hutch illusion, bridge the gap between the upper shelves and lower cabinets with a beaded-board backsplash flanked by side panels and decorative brackets cut from 1× lumber. Add charm to the lower doors, drawers, side pieces, and brackets with simple painted designs, such as crosshatching, dots, and plaid patterns. To give the motifs a worn look, dip an artist's brush into red paint, then into glazing liquid to slightly thin the paint before applying the design. To add decorative scalloped edging to the shelves, see *Shelf Expression, Project 2*.

2 Shelf Expression

Scalloped detailing transforms ordinary shelves into an eye-catching focal point.

- Old cabinets may not be square, so measure the length of each shelf. Cut 1× pine to length and use a template to trace an even scallop, curve, or zigzag design onto the wood. Use a jigsaw or band saw to cut out the design, *Photo A*. Sand the edges, and wipe clean.

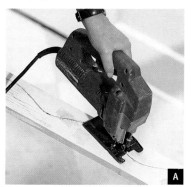

- Brush on primer; let dry. Apply one coat of latex enamel paint; let dry. Use an artist's brush to outline the edges of the pine piece, *Photo B*. Apply simple freehand motifs, or, if you prefer, lightly pencil on the design before painting, or use stencils. For a worn look, dip the brush into paint, then into glazing liquid to slightly thin the paint. Let dry.

- Apply wood glue to the back of the pine. Align pine piece with front edge of the shelf; check position with a carpenter's level. Secure with finishing nails, *Photo C*.

3 Spoon Hardware

Spoons are the perfect size and shape to make drawer pulls. Start with a trip to the flea market where you can find old mismatched silverware quite inexpensively. Transform the spoon into a door or drawer pull by drilling through the scoop and the handle, slightly bending the handle to create a low arch, and screwing the spoon to the door. Choose screws long enough to go through the silverware and about $\frac{3}{8}$ inch into the cabinet door. You can use the same method on a fork, but drill just below the tines and through the bottom of the handle.

Paint and fabric were used to redesign this kitchen inspired by Scandinavian country designs.

Scandinavian Influence continued

4 Painted Plates

These painted-on versions of collectible plates add color and interest and won't ever break or gather dust. The source of inspiration for your plate could be a real plate, a fabric pattern, or a design from a book.

- After the base coat of latex wall color dries, position a real plate in the desired location, and trace it with a pencil. Fill in the outline with white latex paint (or whatever background color you choose) and let dry.
- Use an artist's brush (or stencils and stencil brushes) and crafts paints to add the design; let dry.
- Protect with two coats of water-base polyurethane.

301 decorating projects & ideas

5 No-Sew Swag

This easy-to-make valance doesn't require a needle and thread.

- Cut 54-inch-wide fabric to a length that's 2½ times the width of the window (including trim). Cut the fabric in half lengthwise so it won't be too bulky later when you tie the large knots. Hem all four edges using iron-on fusible webbing.
- Cut a pine 1×2 to match the width of the window, including trim. Find the center of the length of the fabric, and staple the edge of the fabric to the back edge of the 1×2's center. Pull fabric taut from the center, and staple remaining fabric along back edge of 1×2 at 1-inch intervals. Screw the board to the trim above the window. At each top corner of the window, tie a large knot in the fabric and allow the remaining fabric to hang down.

6 Red Shutters

These shutters work well with the swag above by allowing plenty of sunlight into the room, but can be closed at night for privacy. First, measure the length and width of your window. Take the measurements to your local home center where you can purchase unfinished shutters. Paint them the color of your choice. After the paint has dried completely, mount them to the inside wall of the window using hinges.

7 Skirted Seat Cushion

This ruffled seat cushion makes a plain chair prettier.

- Trace the shape of the seat onto kraft paper; cut out. Trace the pattern twice onto decorator fabric, add ½ inch all the way around for seam allowance, and cut out. Trace the pattern twice again onto coarse, stiff batting (for filler), but cut slightly inside the marked lines so the pieces will fit inside the sewn fabric cover.

- To make piping, cover soft cord with bias-cut fabric strips as follows: Fold 1 square yard of fabric diagonally, wrong side out, to form a triangle. With fabric marker, draw a line 1¼ inches from the fold. Mark additional parallel lines 2½ inches apart. Cut out these strips until they are less than a foot long; discard remnants. Align short diagonal ends of strips, and sew with right sides together to form a long, straight casing strip. With casing wrong side up, lay cord along the center. Fold casing over cord, pin, and stitch close to cord, using a sewing machine with a zipper-foot attachment.
- Lay a seat piece flat with right side up. Pin piping around edges, aligning raw edges and overlapping ends; stitch ½ inch from edges.
- To make ruffle, measure perimeter of piped seat piece. Cut fabric to a length double the perimeter measurement (to allow for gathering) and 7½ inches wide. Sew two rows of gathering stitches about ⅛ inch and ¼ inch from one long edge. Pull gathering stitches to form ruffle. Pin ruffle to piped seat piece, aligning raw edges and adjusting gathers evenly to fit; baste in place. With right sides together, pin unpiped seat piece to piped and ruffled piece, sandwiching ruffle and piping between layers and aligning raw edges. Using ½-inch seam allowance, sew through all layers, leaving a wide opening at back of seat cover. Turn right side out, and insert double layer of batting. Pin pairs of ties to cushion where you want to tie it to chair back. Catch the ties' raw edges in the seat-cover opening and hand-stitch opening closed.

8 Etched Glass

Etched verticle stripes add a dash of visual interest to ordinary plain glass cupboard doors.

- Remove the glass from the door frame. Thoroughly clean and dry the glass, and lay it flat on a protected work surface.

Materials

- Glass cleaner
- Etching cream
- Measuring tape
- Foam applicator
- Disposable gloves
- Safety goggles
- Bucket
- Paper towels
- Dishwashing soap
- Water
- Masking tape in a width that matches the distance you want between the etched stripes

- Apply vertical strips of masking tape, leaving space between to etch the stripes. Press edges of tape firmly to the glass using your thumbnail.
- Wearing gloves and goggles, use the foam applicator to apply a thick, even coat of etching cream between the strips of tape. Allow cream to set according to manufacturer's directions (about 15 minutes). Use paper towels to wipe cream off. Rinse any residue from gloves. To give the stripes a more frosted appearance, you can paint them with white paint thinned with glaze or use spray paint in a frosted-glass formula.
- Wash the glass in dish soap and warm water. Remove masking tape, and polish the glass with glass cleaner and lint-free rags or paper towels.
- Reinstall the glass within the door frame so the etched surface faces the interior of the cabinet.

Slipcovers are a great way

1 Basic Slipcover

The basic bodies of these slipcovers are nearly identical—only fabric and embellishments set each slipcover apart.

- It's a good idea to make a muslin pattern before you attempt the actual slipcover so you can double-check fit before cutting into decorator fabric. Add 4 to 6 inches to each measurement to make it easy to pin the pieces together, then sketch the pieces needed on a cutting diagram to determine how many yards of muslin you'll need. (Muslin usually comes in 45-inch widths.) Press the muslin with a clothes iron, if necessary.

- Use a fabric-marking pencil or pen and the measurements for each component to draw pattern pieces onto the muslin. Label each piece (front, back, skirt, etc.), then use a straightedge to mark the vertical center of each. Cut out pieces with fabric scissors or use a rotary cutter and cutting mat. Place each muslin pattern piece on the corresponding part of the furniture, aligning the marked centers and smoothing toward the edges. Loosely pin each piece to the adjoining pieces until all pieces are pinned together, *Photo A.* (Note: There will be several inches of fabric outside the pinned lines.) Step back from the furniture to check the fit, then make any necessary adjustments.

- When you're satisfied with the fit, mark the pinned lines on the muslin, *Photo B.* Remove the muslin from the furniture, remove the pins, and draw a second line ½ inch outside all of the marked lines for seam allowances. Cut out each muslin component along the outer lines.

- Lay out the decorator fabric right side up, press it with a clothes iron, and arrange the muslin pattern pieces— marked side up—on the straight, or lengthwise, grain. If you want, center the fabric's large motifs on the back or seat piece. Pin muslin and decorator fabric together, *Photo C,* then cut out, *Photo D.* Label each piece on the wrong side with fabric pencil.

- Align the raw edges of two adjacent pieces (like the front and the seat) with right sides together, and sew using a ½-inch seam allowance, *Photo E.* Continue until all pieces are stitched together.

- Turn the cover inside out, then slip over the chair. Mark where the hem should fall at several places along the bottom edge, then remove the slipcover. Press with a clothes iron along the marked hem line, and cut the fabric 2 inches beyond the pressed line. To hem, press under 1 inch twice, and sew in place. Trim corner seams to reduce bulk, press seams open, then turn the slipcover right side out. Slip the cover over the chair.

2 Drop Waist

A homemade flower and drop waist add a designer touch to this slipcover.

- Sew the back piece so it doesn't reach the floor.
- Measure and cut a skirt piece so it covers all four sides of the chair.
- Complete the top part of the slipcover first, then pin the skirt as shown, *below*, and sew.
- Embellish with a homemade flower. Coil grosgrain ribbon in a spiral, pinch it into a bundle at the bottom, and hand-stitch through the layers. Tuck raw ends inside to hide them, and pin flower to the slipcover, *below right*.

3 Pleats

Pleats are easy to add—they're mere folds of fabric.

- To add a 1-inch pleat to your slipcover, add 4 inches to the width of the fabric piece that will be pleated, then cut your decorator fabric. With a T-pin, mark the spot where you want the pleat. Measure 2 inches to the right of the T-pin, and create a crease in the fabric, folding that spot back to the T-pin and pinning in place. Repeat on the left side of the T-pin.
- Sew pleated piece to adjacent slipcover pieces. Make a tidy tab, if you'd like, in the desired size and shape, press raw edges under ¼ inch, center tab over the pleat, and topstitch the perimeter.
- Pin a bundle of velour pansies to the tab for an extra flounce, *below*.

4 A Tailored Ruffle

Embellish your slipcover with a tailored ruffle.

- To add a tailored ruffle along one edge, measure the distance the ruffle will span, multiply by 1½ or 2 for folds, then add seam allowances.
- Cut a strip of decorator fabric as long as your determined measurement and twice as wide as the finished width, plus 1 inch (this finished strip is 1 inch wide). Press under long edges ½ inch, press strip in half lengthwise to conceal raw edges, and topstitch along the open side.
- Position ruffle strip along the desired edge of the slipcover, pinning one short, raw edge to a slipcover seam allowance. Situate your needle in the center of the strip width, pinching the fabric into ½-inch folds and stitching down the folds as you sew through all layers, *below top*.
- Pin second raw edge to a slipcover seam allowance, and sew the raw edges into the seams when stitching the slipcover together.

Material Matters

Although you could tediously plot every detail of a slipcover, it's much easier to fit and pin. Take some rough measurements and determine how much yardage you'll need. A slipcover for an average club chair, for example, requires 8 to 10 yards of fabric. You'll need extra fabric for arm covers, piping, loose cushions, throw pillows, and skirts. (For a tailored skirt, measure from the base of the chair to the floor, then double the fabric to give the skirt weight.) If the fabric has a wide pattern repeat, buy extra fabric to make sure the patterns match up.

Approach the piece section by section. Lay fabric over the back of the chair, making sure patterned fabric is straight and centered. Pin the fabric and cut it, leaving ample seam allowances. When cutting, be generous. If you leave too much fabric, it doesn't matter; if you cut away too much, you'll have to start over.

Next, lay fabric over the arms and cut those pieces. Take cues from the chair's upholstery, and follow the original seam placement.

It's best to cut adjacent pieces, stitch them together into a section, and fit as you go. After smaller sections of the cover are sewn, attach those portions to each other. For example, sew together the pieces for the arm before sewing the entire arm to the entire back.

5 Comfortable Classic

Don't give up on your favorite chair if the fabric is worn and faded. Slipcover it and move it into your dining room for an added reading area.

• Make separate slipcovers for the main part of the chair and the cushion. Use medium-weight quilted fabric and piping made to match. A gathered skirt adorned with pom-pom fringe adds a fun detail.

• In lieu of buttons on the chair back, roll three-ball lengths of fringe, tack each with a stitch, and tuft them to the slipcover.

6 Fringe and Ribbon Trim

Ribbon ties and fringe add a hint of frill to this chair.

• Lighten the wood frame with spray paint, then use steel wool to "wear" the paint in places. Add a few coats of clear polyurethane to provide durability to the finish.

• Since the fabric is sheer and features an etching-like pattern, choose a slightly darker underlining fabric that will show off the print.

• To make the ribbon trim, use the same ribbon as for the ties. Pin 2½- to 3-inch loops of ribbon to bias tape, top them with another piece of bias tape, and machine-stitch. Then sew the trim to the bottom of the slipcover as you would any other fringe.

Layers of Fabric

This tailored topper borrows styling from a Swedish pinafore, complete with dual layers of fabric, crocheted lace near the top, piping at the seams, and a gracefully arched hem edged with pretty ribbon.

- Choose medium-weight taupe and cream gingham and ivory linen to give the chair a look that's elegant and understated. To ensure a smooth ribbon border, don't arch the hem too deeply. (A few gathers help the ribbon lie flat.)
- If your machine doesn't do monograms, have one made on a separate piece of fabric. Position the monogram so it's centered from side to side, but slightly higher than center from top to bottom.
- Use hook-and-loop fastening tape to close the cover at the back; this will encourage a forgiving and wrinkle-free fit that's less likely to shift.

Box Pleat

No chair is too old to wear a short skirt.

- Rub white acrylic paint on the chair frame and wipe it off in places to lighten the look without making the chair appear brand new. Apply a coat or two of clear polyurethane to protect the finish.
- Using light- to medium-weight fabric, fashion the skirt into a standard box-pleat design.
- Create the trim from contrasting fabric strips cut on the bias. To give the skirt and bows their shape, slip lightweight floral wire between the fabric layers.
- Place a loose foam pad on the seat beneath the skirt to add softness.

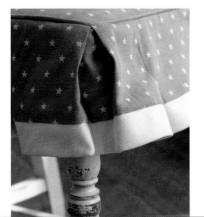

kitchens + dining rooms

Creative Repurposing

1 Gooseneck Chandelier

The dining room chandelier is made from electrical goosenecks, standard light sockets, and colored lightbulbs. The goosenecks, often used for desk lamps, can be purchased from an electrical supply company. The fixture's dome is made of spun aluminum; a restaurant-size colander would achieve a similar effect. Check with local building officials for code requirements. If you're unfamiliar with electricity and wiring, have an electrician wire the fixture for you.

2 Gurney Dining Table

A new top transforms a hospital gurney into a dining room table.

Materials
- Hospital gurney
- Birch or maple plywood, 1 sheet, cut to size appropriate for gurney
- Drywall screws
- $\frac{3}{16}$-inch (inside diameter) flat washers
- Maple or birch 1×2 edging (lengths determined by size of plywood and gurney)
- Wood glue
- Polyurethane varnish

- Purchase an old hospital gurney from a medical supply store or contact your local hospitals' purchasing supply department. Attach plywood to the gurney from underneath by inserting drywall screws through existing holes in the gurney frame, then screwing them into the wood top. Flat washers add support under the screw heads.
- Finish off the edges of the tabletop by gluing solid maple 1×2 edging around the perimeter of the plywood and clamping it in place for 24 hours.
- Sand it flush with the plywood and coat the entire top and edges with a polyurethane varnish.

3 Stacking Cabinet

This stacked cabinet is easy to make and moves from room to room to store odds and ends. To make, visit flea markets, secondhand shops, and garage sales and start a collection of mismatched drawers. Build individual boxes from $\frac{3}{4}$-inch plywood to house each drawer. Mount the largest box on casters. Place the drawers inside the boxes and stack from largest to smallest.

4 Window Wall

A window wall made from salvaged windows can be used to separate rooms while allowing space to flow.

Materials
- 2×4s for wall frame (number and length depend on size of wall)
- Wood-frame windows (number depends on wall)
- Drywall screws
- Paint

- Build a frame with the 2×4s and drywall screws.
- Secure the frame pieces to the existing wall, ceiling, and floor with drywall screws.
- Attach the windows to the frame and to each other with drywall screws, starting at the bottom and working up.
- Paint the wood framing the color of your choice.

5 Photographer's Lights

Old photographer's lights, found at a local secondhand shop, add a fun touch when used as floor lamps.

6 Bowling-Pin Table

An antique metal suitcase doubles as a tabletop and storage compartment. Old bowling pins add a bit of whimsy.

Materials
- Four bowling pins (check thrift stores, garage sales, and bowling alleys)
- Suitcase
- $1\frac{1}{2}$-inch drywall screws
- Washers

- Attach the antique metal suitcase to bowling pins using long drywall screws and washers.

With a little ingenuity, you can turn salvaged and

repurposed materials into attractive furnishings.

7 Pendent Light Fixtures

These pendent light fixtures, an inexpensive find at a flea market, are perfect for task lighting.

Materials
- Porcelain light sockets
- Sheathed electrical cables
- Clip-on tin shades
- Light bulbs

- Wire porcelain light sockets to sheathed electrical cables. The tin shades, which can be found at a flea market or secondhand shop, are held on by the lightbulbs.
- Check with local building officials for code requirements. If you are unfamiliar with electricity and wiring, have an electrician wire the fixture for you.

8 Window Cabinets

These wall-hung upper cabinets started out as windows salvaged from an old building. To make, build plywood boxes to fit the windows and use hinges from your local home center to connect the windows to the boxes. Paint the cabinets the color of your choice. Mount solidly as you would any kitchen cabinet.

9 Barstools

Turn old school chairs into bar stools. To make the chairs taller, insert a length of ¾-inch electrical conduit inside each hollow chair leg. Then pop the glides from the original chair feet onto the ends of the conduit to finish off the legs.

10 Refinish Floors

If solid wood floors are in poor condition, they can be sanded back to their original state. You'll need to rent an upright drum sander for sanding open areas and a disk edge sander for spots the drum sander can't reach.

- Remove all room furnishings, including window treatments.
- Pry off baseboard shoe moldings. Set popped nails below the floor surface. Make any necessary floor repairs, such as filling holes, nicks, and dents. Clean the floor of sticky material that will clog the sandpaper. Remove anything that might tear the sandpaper.
- Seal all outlets, switches, heating ducts, and cold air returns with duct tape and plastic. Mask off doorways with damp sheets or plastic to contain dust. Wear a dust mask, goggles, and ear plugs while working. Use proper ventilation.
- Start off with the drum sander. It's important to keep the sander moving so it doesn't damage the floor by creating a depression where you stop. Tilt the sander back to lift the sandpaper off the floor before turning the sander on and at the end of each pass. For most floors, three sandpaper passes, going with the grain, will smooth the floor. Use rough sandpaper for the first pass, medium for the second, and fine for the third. After each sanding pass, vacuum the floor thoroughly. Use a tack cloth to pick up remaining dust.
- After sanding each pass with the drum sander, use the disk edge sander to do the edges of the floor. As with the drum sander, turn on the edge sander before setting it down and keep it moving at all times.
- Apply paste wood filler with the grain. When the filler begins to set, wipe across the grain with an old rag to remove any excess. Let dry overnight.
- Clean the floor with a tack cloth. Apply two to four coats of polyurethane with a brush, sanding with fine sandpaper between coats. Use a tack cloth to pick up all the dust between coats.

A New Attitude

1 Roman Shade

Tabs and a decorative rod set off this Roman shade made from contrasting fabrics.

- Measure the window as you would for a single-fabric shade. Add an additional inch to the overall fabric length. For example, if your finished shade will be 36 inches long, the full length of both fabrics before sewing will be 47½ inches: 36 inches for the main fabric, 10½ inches of a contrasting fabric, plus 1 inch for the seam allowance between fabrics.
- Sew the two fabrics together with a ½-inch seam.
- To make tabbed edges, cut 3-inch wide bias strips and cut the strips into 6-inch lengths. With right sides together, fold each tab lengthwise. Use a ½-inch seam allowance, and stitch the long edges together. Press the seam open. Turn each tab to the right side. Center the seam on the back of the tab. Press flat.
- When all tabs are complete, fold each in half widthwise, with the seam inside and the raw edges matching. Lay the shade front right side up. Place 1 tab at each edge of the curtain front and evenly space the remaining tabs between these, using 5 to 6 tabs total.
- Using a ½-inch seam allowance, stitch facing to the front of the shade. Press the seam open, with the tab ends toward the facing and the loops toward the shade front. Working from the right side of the fabric, understitch the facing ⅛ inch from the seam, catching the seam allowance of the tabs in the stitching. Turn the facing to the wrong side of the shade front, allowing tabs to pop up. Press.
- Continue making the shade according to the instructions for the *Basic Roman Shade, page 88*. Insert decorative metal rod through tabs after shade is mounted.

2 Countertops

Instead of replacing existing countertops, cover them with stainless steel.

- Draw a template of the countertop size and the sink placement and take it to a metal fabricator. Be sure to ask for a stainless-steel cap to fit over the existing counters.
- Pop out the sink, spread construction adhesive on the metal cap's underside, and fit the cap over the laminate counters just like a shoebox lid.

3 Tile Insets

Draw attention away from outdated tiles by replacing a few of them with delightful fancy glass tile insets.

- Remove the old tiles by breaking each one with a hammer. Use a putty knife to pry underneath.
- Install the glass mosaic tiles with mastic, then grout over them.
- After 15 minutes, wipe off grout residue with a damp sponge.

An outdated kitchen receives an inexpensive makeover using a little paint, stainless steel, and glass tile.

4 Metal Recipe Holder

Display your favorite recipes on this practical magnetic holder.

- Determine the desired length of the metal recipe holder, then add 8 inches. (The width should be 4 to 6 inches, depending on your space.)
- Have a metal fabricator cut a strip of magnetic metal to size. Ask the fabricator to punch a screw hole a couple of inches from each short end, then bend the metal 4 inches from each end. (The flaps should fit flush against the wall and not be visible when the holder is installed.)
- Use a drill with a screwdriver tip to screw the holder to the wall (preferably

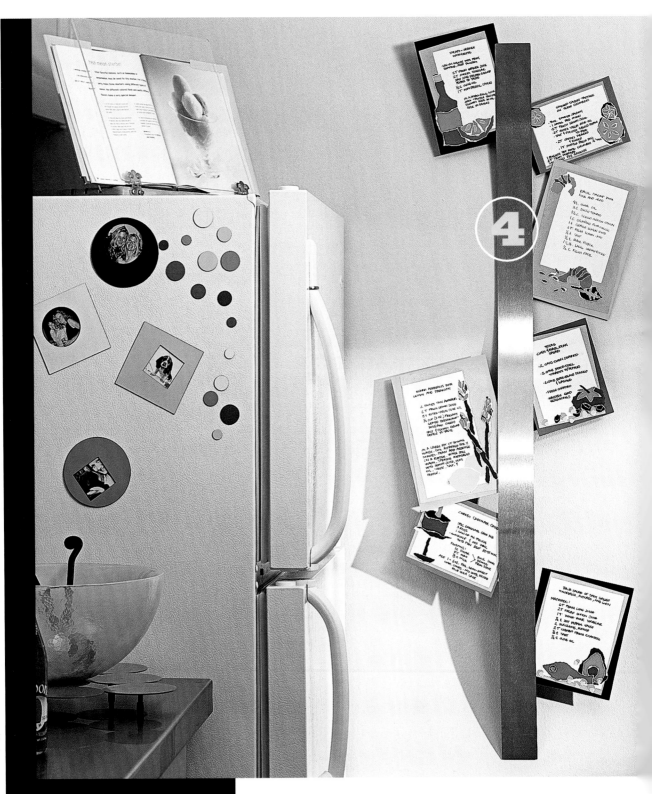

into a stud) through the punched holes. Make sure the metal is slightly curved before you secure it to the wall.
• Use magnets on the underside of the metal strip to hold recipes in place.

5 Freehand Fun

Images of bowls, cups, and saucers personalize plain kitchen cupboards and make it easy to guess what's behind each door. To achieve this look, simply draw images freehand using acrylic paint, available at your local crafts supply store. Don't strive for perfection; vary the width of the lines.

6 Kitchen Shelves

You can make these simple shelves out of items available at your local home center for just a few dollars each.
• Determine how long the shelves should be. For each shelf, cut one pine 1×4 and three pine 1×2s to length. Sand any rough edges.
• Assemble the boards as shown in the diagram, *below*, then fasten them with wood glue, 4d finishing nails, and clamps. Let dry.
• Apply primer first, then paint with a brush, allowing the paint to dry between coats. Secure the shelf to the wall (preferably into studs) with corner braces and appropriate hardware.
• To make wider shelves, simply choose wider lumber such as 1×6 or 1×8. To display heavier items, you may need a more substantial anchor. If you plan to paint, not stain, the shelves, you can opt for paint-grade wood to save money.

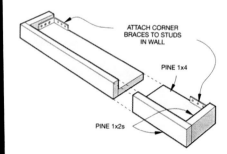

ATTACH CORNER
BRACES TO STUDS
IN WALL

PINE 1x4

PINE 1x2s

Make an Old Kitchen Look New

1 Simple Valance

A cotton leaf-motif print valance tops the window and complements the soft green and white color scheme. The simple valance is an ideal way to take advantage of a fabric remnant or a bit of vintage linen. The fabric width is only slightly wider than the window for the gentle drape between rings. A tailored treatment measures the width of the window plus 1-inch seam allowance for hem. For a fuller look, the width of the window is doubled for the valance. To mount the valance, see the instructions for the *Valance Hardware, Project 6*.

2 Dress a Cabinet Door

This artichoke motif was painted freehand, but you can achieve the same look using the simple pattern, *right*.

- Enlarge the image to the desired size using a photocopier. Scribble on the reverse side of the photocopy using a graphite pencil. Lay the paper on the surface you plan to paint, graphite side down, and tape it in place. Transfer the image to the surface by tracing over the outline with a pencil, then remove the paper. Use acrylic paints and an artist's brush to fill in the outline with color. If you wish, finish by outlining the image with a black paint pen.
- To try painting freehand, study the photograph and follow these suggestions: Paint the white plate first, then shade it with gray. Use a medium-green stripe to better define the shape of the plate. Next paint the shape of an artichoke using one medium tone of green. Apply darker green shading and lighter green highlights as needed.
- Protect your artwork with one or two coats of clear water-base polyurethane sealant.

3 Grooved Dishwasher

The dishwasher was given a fresh look using narrow tongue-and-groove strips.

- Cut the tongue-and-groove strips to length. Round exposed edges with a sander, if desired.
- Paint both sides with primer; let dry. Paint one side in desired color; let dry.
- Using a durable, waterproof adhesive, such as Liquid Nails, glue the strips to the dishwasher front one by one.

4 Grooved Backsplash

Add beauty to your backsplash by surfacing it with narrow tongue-and groove strips. To complete, use the project directions for the *Grooved Dishwasher, Project 3*.

1 SQUARE = 1 INCH

5 Open Storage

Hang window treatment rods on the backsplash along with bent-fork hooks to create open storage. Purchase silver-tone window treatment rods. Screw cup hooks into the bottoms of the upper cabinets and thread fabric strips through the hooks. Tie fabric off to support each end of the rod. Bend forks into hook shapes by holding the end of a fork with a pair of pliers. Bend the handle around needle-nose pliers to create a curve.

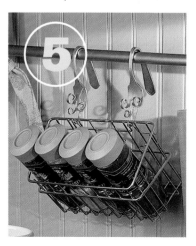

6 Valance Hardware

To match the bent-fork hooks used in the open storage system, forks also act as hardware for the valance. Purchase silver-tone rods and mount using finishing screws. Bend forks by holding the end of a fork with a pair of pliers. Bend the handle around needle-nose pliers to create a curve.

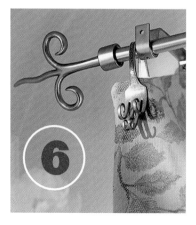

kitchens + dining rooms

7 Laminate Countertop

Plastic laminate comes in 4×8-foot sheets that you can glue to substrate to make your own countertops.

- Form a substrate using two pieces of ¾-inch plywood cut to size. (Make the substrate ¾ inch wider than the cabinet to allow overhang.) Glue and screw one sheet on top of the other to form a 1½-inch-thick surface. (Predrill before screwing, and countersink screws.) Add a 1×2 edge, using glue and 6d finishing nails; countersink nails. Clamp and let dry overnight.
- Using a table saw, cut laminate face up. Begin with countertop edges, cutting laminate strips ½ inch wider than the substrate edge to allow a margin of error. Brush water-base contact cement on both the substrate edges and the backs of the laminate strips, working with one strip at a time, *Photo A*.
- When cement appears cloudy and is dry to the touch, visually align a laminate strip along an edge and press it into place, *Photo B*. If the strip is very long, you may need a helper. Once the glued surfaces touch, it is impossible to lift the laminate and reposition it, so align carefully.
- Use a laminate roller, available at hardware stores, to compress the strip uniformly to the wood edge, *Photo C*.
- After all laminate edges are in place, use a router to trim the laminate to

about ¹⁄₁₆ inch above the top of the countertop substrate surface, *Photo D*.
- Use a belt sander outfitted with 100-grit sandpaper to bring the edge flush with the countertop substrate, *Photo E*.
- Cut the laminate top piece 1 inch longer and wider than the substrate. Apply contact cement to the top of the substrate and the bottom of the laminate. Once cement appears cloudy and is dry to the touch, lay venetian blind slats or thin pieces of wood side by side across the substrate, *Photo F*. Have someone assist you in aligning the laminate atop the substrate using the blind slats as a temporary barrier between the two glue-covered surfaces.
- Once the laminate is properly aligned with the substrate, start at one end, lift a corner of the laminate, and remove three or four slats. Lay the laminate down so the glued surfaces in that corner come into contact. Continue working in the same direction, removing several slats at a time and pressing the countertop into place as you work.
- Run the laminate roller over the entire laminate top. To create a bevel where the laminate top meets the laminate edges, use a router with a tapered bit equipped with a roller bearing at the bottom.
- When finished, attach countertop to cabinets using 1½-inch No. 8 screws.

A

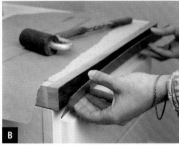
B

C

D

E

F

7

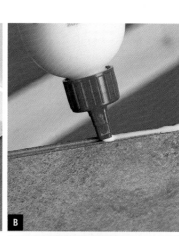

9 Appliquéd Floorcloth

To continue the artichoke theme in the kitchen, artichokes were appliquéd onto a floorcloth. For directions on how to paint a floorcloth, see *Painted Floorcloth, page 45*. You may paint the artichokes (or any design of your choice) freehand, or you can trim the design from a piece of fabric using sharp fabric scissors. To appliqué designs onto the cloth, apply fabric glue to the back of each piece and position on the canvas. Burnish the fabric from the center to the outside edges, expelling any excess glue and air bubbles. Wipe away visible glue. Repeat for remaining fabric pieces. Let dry completely before applying polyurethane.

8 Floating Floor

This laminate floor is installed to float, which means the tiles are glued to one another but not to the subfloor.

- Before you start, if your existing floor is in poor condition, you must remove it before laying new tiles. In many cases, however, laminate flooring can be installed directly over an existing floor made of vinyl, wood, ceramic tiles, or some grades of glue-down commercial carpet. Your flooring manufacturer can help you decide whether to tear up your old flooring.
- Most manufacturers also provide complete instructions so you can install a laminate floor yourself. They can sell you the glue for joining the pieces together, as well as some tools and materials to make the job easier, such as foam padding and spacers, which keep the flooring at least ¼ inch from the walls to allow for expansion.
- Start in a corner by laying down a row of foam padding. Adjust for uneven walls by using a straightedge nailed down over the padding. Position the first tile with the two groove sides facing into the corner, *Photo A*. To continue, position tiles next to one another with a tongue side facing out and a groove side facing the walls.

A

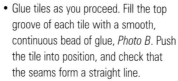

B

- Glue tiles as you proceed. Fill the top groove of each tile with a smooth, continuous bead of glue, *Photo B*. Push the tile into position, and check that the seams form a straight line.
- Use a plastic putty knife to remove excess glue; then wipe the seam with a clean, damp rag, *Photo C*. Continue laying tiles in the same manner, putting glue on the grooved edges. Because the floor floats, there will be a small amount of space between the edge of the tile and the wall, which will be hidden with baseboard molding.

C

Functional Sophistication

1 Slipcovered Chairs

These chairs have been slipcovered in a muslin fabric that picks up the stimulating colors in the sisal carpet. To make similar slipcovers, follow the project instructions for the *Basic Slipcover, page 68*. Because the slipcovers shown here allow part of the chair leg to show, adjust your fabric measurements and allow 1 inch for a hem.

Galvanized pipes and birch plywood combine to make a contemporary statement.

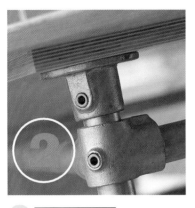

2 Dining Table

This table, made from galvanized pipe and birch plywood, is easy to build after a trip to the home center.

Materials

- One piece ¾-inch birch plywood, 74×48 inches for tabletop (A)
- One piece ¾-inch Baltic birch plywood or conventional birch plywood (see *Baltic Birch Plywood, page 89*), 48×30 inches, for subtop (B)

From 1-inch (inside diameter) galvanized pipe, cut with a hacksaw:

- Four legs (C), 25½ inches long
- Two side braces (D), 40¼ inches long
- Two end braces (E), 22¼ inches long

Other components:

- Polyurethane
- Eight #61-6 Kee Klamp flanges
- Four #21-6 Kee Klamp 90-degree side outlet tees
- No. 10×¾-inch flathead sheet metal screws
- No. 6×1¼-inch deck or drywall screws

• Start by marking with a pencil a 74×48-inch rectangle on a sheet of ¾-inch plywood for the tabletop (A) on the lower-grade face of the wood (look for mismatched veneers or small pin knots). This face will be the underside, but work with it up for now. To create a perfectly shaped oval, measure and scribe the centerlines of the plywood's length and width, see *Diagram A*. Starting at the center point where the lines intersect, measure and mark 28³⁄₁₆ inches in each direction of the lengthwise centerline, then insert a pin or hammer in a small nail at each mark. Cut a 130⅜-inch length of string; tie one end to each pin or nail to create a loop. Starting on the left side of the tabletop, place the pencil point within the string loop and move the pencil around the plywood, keeping string taut and allowing it to guide you. When one side of the oval is marked, pick up the string loop, shift it to the opposite side of the tabletop, and repeat the process to mark the rest of the oval. To help you align the subtop with the tabletop during final assembly, use a measuring tape and the centerlines to mark a 48×30-inch rectangle, centered inside the oval outline you just drew.

• Use a jigsaw to cut out the oval top, being sure to cut just outside the marked line. Sand away the remaining waste material to the line. Using a router equipped with a bearing-guided chamfer bit, rout a ½-inch chamfer on the edge of the tabletop as shown, *left*. Keep in mind that the tabletop is still upside down.

• Finish-sand tabletop and subtop (B). Drill ³⁄₁₆-inch holes (for screws) near each edge of the subtop, about 8 inches apart. Brush both sides of the tabletop and subtop with at least two coats of polyurethane, sanding lightly between coats. Let dry while you assemble the other components.

• File off sharp or rough edges on the legs (C), side braces (D), and end braces (E).

• To assemble the base, see *Diagram B*, start by installing a flange on one (upper) end of each leg. Slide the outlet tee fittings onto the legs so the fittings butt against the flange. Tighten the set screws with a hex key wrench. Install the side braces (D) between pairs of legs, then add the end braces (E) to the assembly. Add the remaining flanges to the lower ends of the legs.

• To assemble the table, see *Diagram B*, first place a blanket or pad on a flat surface. On the blanket, place the tabletop (good face down), then the subtop, then the assembled pipe-and-fitting base. Center the base on the subtop, and align the subtop with the rectangle you drew on the underside of the tabletop in the first step. Attach the base to the subtop with sheet metal screws. Use 1¼-inch deck or drywall screws to fasten the subtop to the tabletop. Set the table right side up.

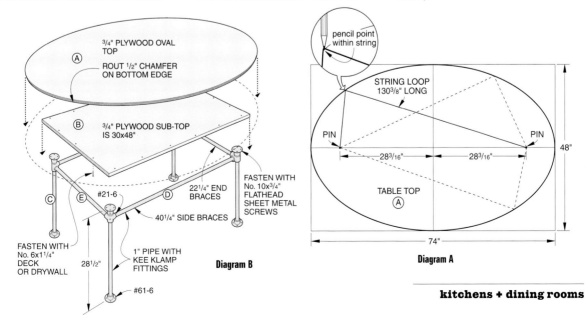

3/4" PLYWOOD OVAL TOP — (A)
ROUT 1/2" CHAMFER ON BOTTOM EDGE
(B) 3/4" PLYWOOD SUB-TOP IS 30x48"
#21-6
22¼" END BRACES
FASTEN WITH No. 10x3/4" FLATHEAD SHEET METAL SCREWS
40¼" SIDE BRACES
FASTEN WITH No. 6x1¼" DECK OR DRYWALL
28½"
1" PIPE WITH KEE KLAMP FITTINGS
#61-6
Diagram B

pencil point within string
STRING LOOP 130³⁄₈" LONG
PIN   PIN
48"
28³⁄₁₆"   28³⁄₁₆"
TABLE TOP (A)
74"
Diagram A

Functional Sophistication continued

3 Wine Rack

This wine rack provides an amazing amount of storage and display for bottles, glasses, and other items.

- Using a table saw, cut a rabbet along the upper and lower edges of each shelf box side panel (G), then cut a ¼-inch-wide rabbet along the rear edge of all the shelf box top panels and bottom panels (F) to accept the ¼-inch plywood shelf box back panels (K), see detail in Diagram B, *opposite*. Glue and clamp the boxes together, then rout a ½-inch chamfer around inside edge of the box opening. Drive 4d finishing nails at the joints to reduce clamping time, if desired.

Countersink the nails with a nail set and fill the holes with wood putty. Apply two coats of polyurethane to plywood components with a paintbrush, letting dry, then sanding lightly between coats.

Materials

From three sheets of ¾-inch Baltic birch plywood or one sheet of regular birch plywood, cut:

- Four shelf box top/bottom panels (F), 31½×16 inches
- Four shelf box side panels (G), 16×14 inches
- Four wine rack top/bottom panels (H), 15½×16 inches
- Four wine rack side panels (I), 16×16 inches

From a half-sheet of ½-inch birch plywood, cut:

- Four wine rack dividers (J), 21½×15 inches

From a half-sheet of ¼-inch birch plywood, cut:

- Two shelf box back panels (K), 31¼×13¼ inches
- Two wine rack back panels (L), 15¼×15¼ inches

From ¾-inch (inside diameter) galvanized pipe, cut with a hacksaw:

- Four legs (M), 66 inches long
- 20 horizontal braces (N), 16¾ inches long

Other components:

- Sixteen #21-5 Kee Klamp 90-degree side outlet tees (see *The Right Fittings, opposite*)
- Four #20-5 Kee Klamp side outlet elbows
- Four #61-5 Kee Klamp flanges
- Wood glue, 4d finishing nails, wood putty, and polyurethane

Note: If this wine rack will sit on thick carpeting or measure over 4 feet in height, we recommend you replace the #61-5 Kee Klamp flange with a #60-5 Kee Klamp flange that has a wider base for additional stability.

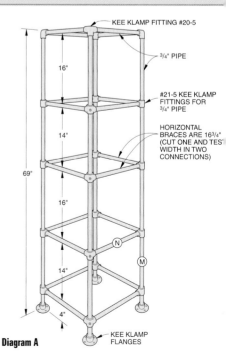

Diagram A

KEE KLAMP FITTING #20-5

¾" PIPE

#21-5 KEE KLAMP FITTINGS FOR ¾" PIPE

HORIZONTAL BRACES ARE 16¾" (CUT ONE AND TEST WIDTH IN TWO CONNECTIONS)

16"

14"

69"

16"

14"

4"

N

M

KEE KLAMP FLANGES

- Repeat the first step to construct wine-rack boxes. With the boxes assembled, check the inside diagonal measurement and cut the wine rack dividers (J) ¹⁄₁₆ inch shorter so they will easily slide into place. Rout a ½-inch chamfer along both sides of the divider ends to reveal the wood's plies, and cut two ¾×7½-inch half-lap notches in their centers. Brush on two coats of polyurethane to dividers, letting dry, then sanding lightly between coats.
- To assemble the base, install a horizontal brace (N) between each of the two pairs of elbow fittings and the eight pairs of tee fittings.
- Install the assembled brace sections on one leg (M), spacing them as indicated, Diagram A, *lower left*. With the elbow and tee fittings locked to one leg, slide another leg into position, forming a ladder; lock the second leg to the fittings. Repeat this process for the two remaining legs.
- With one ladder lying on a flat surface, fittings pointed up, install the remaining braces. Fit the other ladder atop the braces. (Note: It may take some minor adjusting of the second ladder assembly to get the fittings and braces to line up properly.)
- Install the flanges on the bottom of the legs. Fit the shelf and wine-rack boxes in the rack, adjusting the spacing between braces as needed.

4 Table Carousel

This lazy Susan holds wine bottles for entertaining and can also be used as a floral centerpiece.

Materials
- Three 14-inch-diameter ¾-inch plywood circles for base (O), lower plate (P), and top plate (Q)
- One ¼-inch-diameter, 20 threads-per-inch (tpi) threaded rod, 40 inches long
- Polyurethane
- One 12-inch-diameter lazy Susan bearing
- Screws to fit lazy Susan apparatus
- Twenty ¼-inch nuts and flat washers

- To determine the placement of the five openings, locate the center point and the top plate (Q) with a measuring tape. From the center point, use a protractor and pencil to mark a radius every 36 degrees, dividing the circle into 10 equal sections. Using the same center point, use a compass with pencil to draw two circles on the top plate—one ¾ inch from the edge and another 2½ inches from the edge (the two circles will be 12½ and 9 inches in diameter, respectively).
- Use a hacksaw to cut the threaded rod into five 8-inch lengths; thread a nut onto the portion you're cutting so you can back it off the end and straighten any threads damaged during cutting. To drill the holes for the threaded rods, first clamp the top plate (Q) and lower

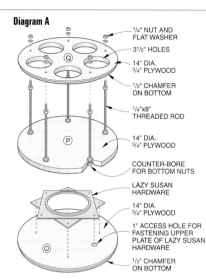

Diagram A

- ¼" NUT AND FLAT WASHER
- 3½" HOLES
- 14" DIA. ¾" PLYWOOD
- ½" CHAMFER ON BOTTOM
- ¼"×8" THREADED ROD
- 14" DIA. ¾" PLYWOOD
- COUNTER-BORE FOR BOTTOM NUTS
- LAZY SUSAN HARDWARE
- 14" DIA. ¾" PLYWOOD
- 1" ACCESS HOLE FOR FASTENING UPPER PLATE OF LAZY SUSAN HARDWARE
- ½" CHAMFER ON BOTTOM

plate (P) together. Drill a ¼-inch hole on every other radius line along the outer marked circle. Unclamp the plates, switch to the hole saw, and drill five 3½-inch holes in the top plate (Q) with the center points on the other five radius lines where the inner circle intersects them. To verify hole locations, see Diagram A, *above*.
- To mount the lazy Susan bearing to the underside of the lower plate (P), drill a 1-inch access hole in the base (O) as indicated. Rout a ½-inch chamfer on the bottom edge of the base and top plate. Drill ¾-inch-diameter counter-bores in the bottom surface of the lower plate to recess the washers and nuts.
- Use a paintbrush to apply two coats of polyurethane to all plywood components, letting dry, then sanding between coats.
- Install the threaded rods, keeping the top and lower plates parallel.
- Mount the lazy Susan bearing to the base (O), then, through the 1-inch access hole, fasten the base to the plate assembly with screws.

The Right Fittings

Putting together the pipe-and-plywood table and wine rack requires special pipe fittings designed for industrial use (90-degree side outlet tees, flanges, and elbows). These are metal joints that let a pipe turn a corner, connect to a wall or floor, or fasten to other unthreaded pipes. This project specifies Kee Klamp fittings from Kee Industrial Products (1-800-851-5181), which distributes its products nationwide. You could also use fittings from another manufacturer; just be sure they fit the pipes you're using before you buy.

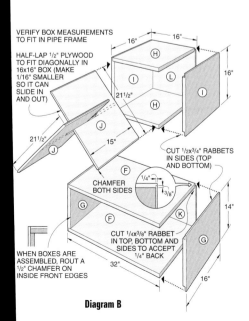

VERIFY BOX MEASUREMENTS TO FIT IN PIPE FRAME

HALF-LAP ½" PLYWOOD TO FIT DIAGONALLY IN 16x16" BOX (MAKE 1/16" SMALLER SO IT CAN SLIDE IN AND OUT)

16"
16"
16"
21½"
21½"
15"
¼"
3/8"

CUT ½"x¾" RABBETS IN SIDES (TOP AND BOTTOM)

CHAMFER BOTH SIDES

CUT ¼"x3/8" RABBET IN TOP, BOTTOM AND SIDES TO ACCEPT ¼" BACK

14"
32"
16"

WHEN BOXES ARE ASSEMBLED, ROUT A ½" CHAMFER ON INSIDE FRONT EDGES

Diagram B

Functional Sophistication continued

5 Painted Walls

The wall has been painted two shades of breezy green to make the room feel more spacious.

- Tape off moldings, trim, and ceiling. Choose your colors and widths. The colors may contrast or be differing values of the same color.
- Prime the walls. Allow the primer plenty of time to dry.
- To apply the top horizontal stripe, start at the top of the wall, and make a series of measurement marks vertically around the room. Use blue painter's tape to mask off the area. Apply the first coat of paint. Remove the tape immediately to avoid lifting the paint off the wall. Allow paint to dry thoroughly.
- To apply the lower color, mask off the area with blue painter's tape. Apply the second coat of paint. Remove the tape immediately and allow the paint to dry.

6 Basic Roman Shade

Roman shades are both elegant and practical. They are perfect for spaces where you want to maximize sunlight and also offer complete privacy at night.

Making the Shade:
- Measure the inside window width and length. This is the finished size of the shade. Add 2 inches to the width and 10½ inches to the length; cut a rectangle of the fabric with these measurements.
- To finish the sides, fold under ½ inch on each side and press, fold ½ inch again, press and seam both sides.
- To finish the top, press under ½ inch, then 2 inches; stitch in place.
- To make the rod pocket, press under 4 inches at the bottom of the shade. Stitch across the width of the shade 1½ inches from the fold to create a rod pocket. Fold up the bottom another 4 inches. Stitch across width near the top fold. When you've finished sewing the rest of the shade and are ready to install it, insert the metal rod or wood dowel in the pocket, slip-stitch closed.
- To attach the ring tape, place the bottom ring of the tape just above

Materials
- Face fabric
- ½ inch wood dowel
- Roman shade ring tape
- 1×2 wood strip, ¼–½ inch shorter than the width of your window (for the mounting board)
- Adhesive-back nylon hook-and-loop tape
- Screw eyes large enough for multiple cording lengths
- Two L-brackets with screws
- Nylon cording
- Awning cleat

the rod pocket. End with the top ring 4 inches from the top of the shade. Make sure the rings are perfectly aligned and stitch around the tape.

Mounting the Shade:
- Press one side of the hook-and-loop fastening tape across the front edge of the mounting board, and the other side of the tape across the top edge on the wrong side of the shade. To mount the shade to the mounting board, press the hook-and-loop fastening tape together.
- Next, mark points on the underside of the mounting board for the placement of screw eyes. The screw eyes must correspond with the vertical row of rings on the shade. Screw the screw eyes to each point.
- To thread rings, see illustration, *right*, cut the nylon cording into lengths that measure the length of a vertical row of rings, plus the width of the shade, plus at least half the length of a vertical row of rings. Cut one length for each vertical row of rings.
- Knot the end of a cord length to the bottom ring of each vertical row. Thread the first (left side) cord length through its vertical row of rings and the corresponding screw eye.
- Thread the next cord length through its vertical row of rings, its corresponding screw eye, and the screw eye to its left.
- Thread the remaining cording lengths in the same manner in order as directed above, threading each length through all of the screw eyes to the left. When all threading is complete, all cording lengths should be threaded through the far-left screw eye. Tie the excess lengths together in a loose knot.
- To mount the shade, see illustration, *right*, secure the mounting board inside the window to the top of the window frame. Secure it with two L-brackets.
- Mount the awning cleat to the right of the window. Pull on the cording lengths to make sure the shade pulls up evenly; then release the shade. Braid the cording lengths together, and knot them at the end. Wrap the braided length around the awning cleat to hold the shade at the desired level.

Two Panels on the Shade's Length:

Multiple fabrics customize a Roman shade. Here's how to measure and cut fabrics when you have two panels on the length of the shade, as in the photo shown.

- Measure the window as you would for a single-fabric shade. Add an additional inch to the overall fabric length. For example, if your finished shade will be 36 inches long, the full length of both fabrics before sewing will be 47½ inches: 36 plus the 10½ inches for the pattern, plus 1 inch for the seam allowance between fabrics.
- First, sew the two fabrics together with a ½-inch seam, and then continue making the shade according to the basic instructions, *opposite*.

Measuring Windows Tips:

- For the most exact measurements, use a steel measuring tape. Decide whether you want your treatments to fit inside the window or to cover the window (an outside mount). Measure accordingly.
- For an inside mount, measure the opening width at the top, middle, and bottom, recording the narrowest measurement. Do the same for the length, recording the longest measurement. Round to the closest ⅛ inch.
- For an outside mount, measure the opening width, and add at least 3 inches to each side of the window opening if space allows. Measure the opening length, and add at least 2 inches in height for hardware and any overlap.
- To measure the drop for draperies, measure your windows from where you install the rod to where you want the draperies to fall. For width, measure the full length of the rod. To calculate the length of a decorative scarf or a single fabric piece, measure the distance from the bottom of the drapery ring or the top of the rod to the desired length of the scarf. Multiply that measurement by 2, and add 10 inches to each side if you want the fabric to puddle on the floor. Measure the width of the area to be covered, and add that figure to the length for the total needed yardage.

7 Painted Sisal Carpet

The sisal carpet adds texture and stimulating color to energize the room. Sisals vary in coarseness, but all soak up paint. If you're using five or six colors on an 8×10-foot rug, plan on a gallon for each color.

- Place a drop cloth under the carpet. There's no need to mask off each stripe: Follow the rug's weave for crisp lines.
- Determine each stripe's width and the placement of each color. Work one stripe at a time when painting the whole rug so each has time to dry to the touch before you paint the next.
- To apply paint, it's easiest to use a paint pad for each color; bristle or foam brushes won't saturate the rug's surface as well. Dip the paint pad into a shallow container of paint, dragging the pad across the container's rim to evenly saturate the pad. Press the pad into the rug's fibers; don't use a brushing motion. Repeat for other stripes and colors.
- Allow the carpet to dry for two to three days before putting it into service.

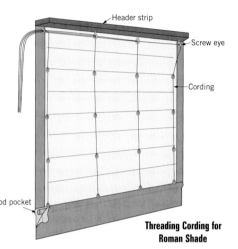

Threading Cording for Roman Shade

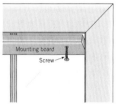

Inside Mount for Roman Shade

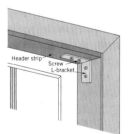

Inside Mount for Roman Shade

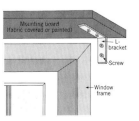

Outside Mount for Roman Shade

Baltic Birch Plywood

The Baltic birch plywood (also called European or Finnish birch) used to build the wine rack, table carousel, and parts of the table is different in size, construction, and availability from conventional birch plywood.

Baltic birch plywood is manufactured in metric sizes, but when sold in the United States, the panels are described with the closest fractional inch size; 6-millimeter panels are sold as ¼-inch plywood, 18-millimeter panels are sold as ¾-inch, and so on. Measure panels before you buy.

Most plywood is sold in 4×8-foot sheets, but Baltic birch panels measure about 5 feet square. Because the sheets are wider and shorter and have less surface area than other plywood, you'll need to lay out project components differently and purchase more sheets.

1 Apple Harvest

A window screen placed behind this cutout leaves the focus on the apple rather than the contents inside the cupboard.

- Remove and clean the existing hardware using steel wool to remove paint and grime.
- Draw the apple shape (or shape of your choice) on construction paper with a

Materials and Tools
- Sandpaper, fine
- Steel wool, fine
- Jigsaw
- Miter saw or wood saw
- Construction paper
- Pencil
- Scissors
- Straightedge
- Paintbrush
- Apple green eggshell-finish latex paint
- Red eggshell-finish latex paint
- Clear satin-finish sealer
- Crackle glaze medium
- Aluminum window screening
- Wood screen molding
- Hammer
- Small wire brads

pencil, then cut the shape out with scissors to create a template.
- Using the template, outline the shape in the desired position on the cabinet door face. Cut out the shape with a jigsaw. Sand the cutout area, face, back, and sides of the door to prepare for painting.
- Apply two coats of apple green eggshell-finish paint to the entire door with a brush. (Paint one side, let dry, turn over, and paint the opposite side.)
- Apply crackle glaze medium, following the manufacturer's instructions. Apply one coat of red eggshell-finish paint, and allow the crackle glaze medium to take effect. Finally apply one coat of clear satin-finish sealer.
- Once the paint has completely dried, turn the door face down. Using the apple template as a guide, cut a square piece of window screening, leaving about 1 inch extra on all sides. Cut four pieces of screen molding to form a frame along the outer edge of the window screen. Paint the four pieces of screen molding, following the same process as for the door.
- Place the window screen over the cutout area, and secure it with the molding and small brads. Turn the door face up, and reattach the previously cleaned hardware.

2 Embossed Designs

A tin-patterned wallpaper spray painted with a metallic silver paint gives this cupboard an embossed look.

Materials and Tools
- Tin-patterned wallpaper
- Heavy-duty wallpaper adhesive
- Metallic silver spray paint
- Black glaze medium
- Sandpaper, fine
- Paintbrush
- Clean, soft cloth
- Utility knife

- Remove the existing hardware. Sand the entire door face.
- Cut the wallpaper to fit the center frame of the cabinet door, making sure the pattern is positioned on center.

- Apply the wallpaper using wallpaper adhesive. Let dry.
- Spray paint the wallpaper with metallic silver paint. Let dry.
- Apply the black glaze medium with a brush, and wipe off using a clean, soft cloth to create an antique effect.
- Apply two coats of khaki eggshell-finish paint (or color of your choice) to the remaining frame and trim.
- Mask off and paint the inside edge of the trim with black semigloss paint. Let dry and remove tape.
- Drill a hole; attach a new pewter knob.

3 Glass Impressions

Rice paper is placed between two glass panels to create this mottled design.

- Remove the existing hardware. Using a circular saw, cut the center panel from the back, approximately ½ inch inside the face frame.
- Measure the new opening, and have two pieces of glass cut to these dimensions at a picture-framing store.
- Miter cut four pieces of molding to fit within the new opening.
- Using wood stain, stain these pieces to match the existing door color.

- When the stain is dry, apply a clear satin finish.
- Sand the remaining face frame, and apply pickling gel with a clear, soft cloth to create the weathered effect. When dry, apply a clear satin finish.
- Cut the rice paper to the size of the glass panels.
- Place the rice paper between the panels, and secure them in the opening, using the molding pieces held in place with small brads.
- Drill a hole and attach a new antique brass leaf knob.

Materials and Tools

- Rice paper
- 2 precut glass panels
- Circular saw
- Sandpaper, fine
- ¼×¼-inch molding
- Wood stain
- Pickling gel
- Clear satin-finish latex
- Paintbrush
- Clean, soft cloth
- Small brads
- Small maple leaf antique brass knob

kitchens + dining rooms

Things to Consider

Before you start a cabinet facelift, assess whether your cabinetry is fit for a redo and how much the makeover will cost. If you're planning to repaint, you'll only have to spend a few dollars for a fresh new look. If you're planning to replace hardware and other trim, consider your options. If you decide to make a change, carefully prepare cabinet doors before adding a new finish:

• Remove doors from their cabinet boxes, and remove hardware. If you're changing hardware, fill the old screw holes with wood filler and sand.

• Make any major repairs, such as regluing loose parts. Fill in holes with wood filler or caulk. Fill gaps where wood pieces have shrunk.

• Examine the finish. It may be worthwhile to strip the old finish to get a smooth base. If not, sand rough spots before you resurface.

• If the surface of the cabinets is smooth and doesn't require any repairs, scrub the cabinets using a heavy-duty cleaner such as TSP (trisodium phosphate). This will remove any greasy residue.

• For painted finishes, coat the surface with a good-quality primer.

Materials and Tools

• 6×6-inch wood plaque
• Carved-wood medallion appliqué
• Adhesive
• Sandpaper, fine
• Wood knob
• Terra-cotta eggshell-finish latex paint
• Black semigloss-finish latex paint
• Gray-green acrylic crafts paint
• Dark terra-cotta glaze medium
• Diamond patterned wallpaper
• Heavy-duty wallpaper adhesive
• Drill
• Screwdriver
• Paintbrush
• Quick-release tape
• Sponge
• Scissors
• Utility knife

4 Carved Wood

A carved-wood medallion provides the inspiration for this cabinet.

- Remove the existing hardware. Sand the entire door.
- Apply the wood plaque and the carved-wood medallion appliqué to the door, using adhesive.
- Paint entire door with two coats of terra-cotta eggshell-finish paint. Mask off and paint the indented border, the edge of the plaque, and the wood knob with two coats of black semigloss paint. Let dry.
- Using a dry brush, stipple gray-green paint lightly onto the black areas. Let dry and remove tape.

- Remask and use a sponge to apply dark terra-cotta glaze medium over the terra-cotta areas. Let dry.
- Cut a piece of wallpaper to fit within the indented border, and cut out the area for the raised plaque. Attach the wallpaper. Let dry.
- Drill a hole and attach the previously painted wood knob.

5 Photo Finish

Personalize your cabinets using your favorite old or new family photographs.

- Select a photo—either an antique or a recent favorite. Take it to a photo-processing store, and have it enlarged

to the desired size with a matte, washable laminate finish.
- Remove the existing hardware, and fill the holes. Sand the entire door.
- Apply two coats of ivory eggshell-finish paint. Create the border using a stencil brush, a stencil, and antique gold paint. Let dry.
- Cut photo to fit within the face frame, and attach with spray-mount adhesive. Let dry.
- Drill a hole and attach a new knob.

Materials and Tools
- Photograph
- Spray-mount adhesive
- Utility knife
- Metal straightedge
- Sandpaper, fine
- Ivory eggshell-finish latex paint
- Stencil
- Stencil brush
- Antique gold paint
- Drill
- Brass knob

301 decorating projects & ideas

baths

Fabric, paint, and fun accessories can transform any bath into a relaxing retreat. Create a stencil using a shower curtain as inspiration. Skirt a vanity in a cottage floral print. Paint a garden of poppies on a tub and medicine cabinet. Repurpose a vintage table into a vanity. Paint a diamond pattern onto a wall. Embellish store-bought towels. Quilt a bath mat. Turn greeting cards into art.

48

projects & ideas

Quaint Bath Retreat

Berry red walls, a poppies motif, and slipcovered furniture combine to make this bath a relaxing retreat.

1 Layered Shower Curtain

A contrasting valance adds a finishing touch to this floral shower curtain. To make the shower curtain, measure the circumference of the shower curtain ring for the fabric width. For the length, measure the distance from the bar to the floor. Cut fabric. Add 2 inches for seams on the top, bottom, and side opening. If you have to use multiple pieces of fabric to get the width, be sure to add 1 inch for each seam allowance. Fold over raw edges and sew to final size. Add grommets at the top and hang using metal shower curtain rings. To make the coordinating valance, cut the fabric the width of the shower curtain and to desired length. Add 2 inches for seam allowances (on top, bottom, and sides). Fold over raw edges and sew to final size. Embellish with giant rickrack along the bottom edge of the valance. Add grommets, and hang from the metal rings with the shower curtain.

6 Skirted Stool

A small stool is skirted to coordinate with the pedestal sink and vanity and extends counter space in the bath. To make, see the instructions for the *Vanity Fabric Cover, Project 12,* and *Vanity Skirting, Project 13.*

7 Terrycloth Bath Mat

A terrycloth bath mat picks up the green and white gingham fabric used throughout the bath. Start with a terrycloth towel in the size and color of your choice. Measure the diameter of the towel, and cut fabric strips to size, adding ½-inch seam allowance. Fold edges under and stitch. Measure the width of the towel, and cut fabric strips, again adding ½-inch seam allowance. Fold edges under and stitch. Stitch the strips in place along the diameter and across the width of the towel. Place nonskid backing under the mat.

Fabric Tips

Follow these tips for choosing and caring for fabrics in a bathroom:

- Consider who will use the bath and how often. In a guest bath or powder room that's rarely used, use a fabric that's more dramatic and less practical. In a child's bath, think practical, such as a laminated fabric shower curtain.
- Keep it natural. Choose only natural fabrics, such as cotton, cotton blend, or linen fabrics.
- Wash natural-fiber fabrics in cool water, dry on low, then smooth out wrinkles with a cool iron.
- Avoid using stain-prone fabrics or ones that require dry cleaning. Poor choices for a bathroom would be silk, which shows water stains, and upholstery-weight fabric, which typically must be dry-cleaned.

2 Painted Tub

A hand-painted garden of poppies brings an old tub to life.
- First remove grime by cleaning tub sides with TSP (trisodium phosphate).
- Apply one coat of latex primer. Let dry.
- Apply one coat of white gloss or semigloss latex paint. Let dry.
- Paint design freehand or use stencils with latex paint or decorative crafts paint. (You can also use a sponge, rag, or combing technique on the outside of the tub.)
- To clean the outside of the painted tub, use a damp sponge and avoid using abrasive cleaners.

3 Medicine Cabinet

A white medicine cabinet accented with hand-painted poppies provides a nice contrast against the berry-red walls.
- Apply one coat of a good-quality latex primer. Let dry.

- Apply one coat of white gloss or semigloss latex paint. Let dry.
- Use latex paint or decorative crafts paint to paint design freehand or use stencils.
- Seal with a polyurethane finish.

4 Poppy Border

A wallpaper border of poppies defines the doorway and complements the fabric used for the shower curtain.

5 Skirted Sink

Pretty green and white gingham fabric skirts a pedestal sink to hide plumbing pipes. To make, see the instructions for the *Vanity Skirting, Project 13.*

baths **97**

Quaint Bath Retreat continued

8 Valance

For this easy window topper, the fabric itself forms a cornice.

- Cut a 3-inch-deep dust board that is as wide as your window. Cut out the fabric to form the face and ends, adding ½ inch to all edges for seams. Cut a fabric lining the same size. Sew the lining to the fabric, with right sides together, leaving an opening for turning right side out.
- Trim the seams, clip the corners, turn and press. Slip-stitch the opening closed. Sew or glue the trim of your choice to the lower edge.

- Center the fabric on the dust board, smoothing front-facing fabric over the top of the board, and staple. Fold the end fabric gift-wrap style over the top for smooth corners.
- Mount the board to the window trim with screws or to the wall above the window using L-brackets.

9 Window Treatment

Poppy-covered fabric paired with green and white gingham makes a sophisticated statement at the window. To make, measure your window. Cut a piece of fabric to fit the size of your window, adding ½-inch seam allowance to all the edges. If you desire, add a contrasting border with fabric tape or ribbon. Nail the corners of the panel to the window frame. Add a valance to hide the nails.

10 Floral Artwork

Framed greeting card and postcard designs make wonderful works of art. For additional ideas, see *Greeting Card Art, page 102*.

11 Simple Vanity

A vanity adds much-needed counter space to this bath.

- To create the tabletop, cut a piece of particleboard or plywood to the desired shape and size.
- For legs, cut 2x4s to the desired length (about 33 to 36 inches), and nail or screw a leg to the bottom of the wood tabletop at each corner. You can also screw cleats to the wall to support the tabletop.

12 Vanity Fabric Cover

A fabric cover conceals the plywood top of this vanity. Cut a piece of fabric the size and shape of the tabletop, adding about 1½ inches all around. Lay fabric right side down on a work surface. Center the tabletop on the fabric, fold excess fabric over the tabletop edges, and staple to secure.

13 Vanity Skirting

A green and white gingham skirting adds softness to this vanity.

- Measure around the vanity from wall to wall. Multiply total measurement by 2½ or 3 to allow enough fabric for pleating. Measure the height of the vanity from where you plan to hang the skirt down to the floor; add 3 inches to allow for top and bottom hems. (A wide hem adds body and weight to the bottom of the skirt.)
- Sew a 2-inch bottom hem and a 1-inch top hem. To pleat the skirt, use a toothpick to push equal amounts of fabric beneath the sewing machine foot and stitch across ¼- to ½-inch-wide pleats. It's easier if you stitch one pleat at a time.

- Cover pleating stitches with jumbo rickrack braiding, cord, or ribbon that you sew or glue on.
- Apply the skirt to the vanity using hook-and-loop tape.

14 Slipcovered Chair

Slipcovers that are made with dressmaker details, such as scalloped edging, lend sophistication to ordinary furnishings in the bath. The slipcover shown is made from a creamy, textured fabric. To make a similar cover, see the project instructions for the *Basic Slipcover, page 68*. To embellish as in the slipcover shown, sew giant rickrack into the seam to create the scalloped edge. Extend the length of the fabric so it drops down 5 or 6 inches from the edge of the rickrack to create a double scalloped look.

15 Pillows

Pillows in a mixture of bright fabrics accent the slipcovered bench in this bath. To make similar pillows to the ones shown, see the instructions for the *Pillows, page 12*. You can embellish the pillows by sewing tassels to the corners as in the pillow shown.

baths

Cottage-Garden Bath

1 Accessories

Vintage and nautical accessories add charm to this cottage-style bath. Starfish dance along a narrow shelf and sit on a vintage blue chair between a collection of seashells and framed art. For additional ideas for displaying vintage and nautical accessories, see *Seafaring Cottage, pages 36–41*.

2 Window Treatment

This simple window treatment is made out of a vintage curtain panel. To make, cut a curtain panel to fit your window. Hem the raw edges. Use strips of antique fabric to accent the curtain and give it shape. (Strips of ribbon will also work.) Cut the fabric to your desired width and hem the raw edges. The strips should be twice the length of the fabric, plus a couple of inches for later adjustment. Stitch ends together and slide over the fabric. Nail the corners of the panel into the cement board. Hide the nailheads with large glued-on buttons.

Vintage flowered fabrics and salvaged items create the cottage-style look of this bath.

3 Crown Molding Shelf

Place crown molding, available at your local home center, on top of the cement-board siding to create a narrow shelf for collectibles. Install the crown molding with finishing nails.

4 Repurposed Vanity

Add country flair by turning a vintage table into a vanity.

- Start with a self-rimming sink to help keep water off the tabletop. If your sink doesn't come with its own template, draw your own and tape it to the table's top. Drill a ¼-inch hole on the inside of the outline, then use a jigsaw to carefully cut along the inside of the template.
- Waterproof the table. For natural wood, sand the wood top lightly using sandpaper with a very fine grit; use a tack cloth to remove all dust. Apply a coat of high-gloss polyurethane. If your piece is painted, protect the top with one or two coats of high-gloss acrylic.
- Once the plumbing has been hooked up by you or a professional, and before the sink has been cemented, slightly adjust the position of the sink as needed. To provide a good seal between the sink and countertop, apply a thin bead of caulk.
- Separate faucet and handles will allow you to install the fixtures on the sides of the bowl, where they're most easily accessible, as in the vanity shown, see *page 102*.

5 Vanity Skirt

Attach a piece of vintage fabric to the underside of the vanity to hide the sink's pipes and allow for storage underneath. To make, see *Vanity Skirting, page 99*.

6 Floral Shower Curtain

Floral sheets were used to make this cottage-style shower curtain. The instructions below are for one curtain panel. You will need two panels for a shower curtain, so double yardage.

- Measure the length of the rod including returns, if any, and from the top of the rod to the floor. The finished width of the curtain equals the length of the rod plus returns. For total length, add 6 inches for hem and casing.
- Seam panels together if necessary to obtain the appropriate amount of fullness. Allow extra yardage for matching repeats or one-way designs.
- Cut the panel and join with French seams. Make a 1-inch finished hem on each side.
- For casing and heading, make a 2-inch finished hem along the top edge. Stitch ½ inch from the top fold to form the heading.
- Make a 3-inch finished hem along the bottom edge.
- Gather panels onto the rod.
- Make simple fabric strips, cut to your desired length, to tie back panels. Hem raw edges. (Strips of ribbon will also work.)

baths

Cottage-Garden Bath *continued*

7 | Enamelware Bowl

An enamelware bowl, hand-painted with roses and leaves, makes an ideal sink in a country-inspired bath. To transform the deep, wide bowl, cover the area with blue masking tape to prevent the paint from chipping. Then drill a drain hole into the base using a carbide-tip drill.

8 | Greeting Card Art

Floral greeting cards and postcards make inexpensive works of art. Museums are a great source for this type of artwork. They sell cards with botanical images as well as art reproduction images. Bookstores are another source. After you have selected a card, purchase a frame and coordinating mat from your local discount or crafts supply store. To prevent damage from moisture, use a frame with glass. Display on a window sill or prop up on a vintage chair as in the photo shown.

9 Cement-Board Siding

Cement board, the kind used for exterior siding, wraps around the walls in this bath. The siding comes in long planks and is completely waterproof. Mount each plank to the wall with screws, then cover the screws with the plank immediately above. Join the boards with caulk in the corners of the room. In the shower stall shown, the siding is stretched 7 feet high, far enough up to protect the wall from splashes. It's a good idea to have the siding professionally installed to ensure a proper fit.

10 Creative Plumbing

Plumbing pipes and fittings make inexpensive hardware in your bath. In the bath shown, two towel bars, a toilet paper holder, and a shower curtain rod were constructed for about the same price as a single chrome towel bar available in stores. The fixtures are each made from nippled plumbing pipe cut to the desired length, 90-degree elbows, and two additional short 1½-inch nipples. Two flanges attach the whole piece to the wall. The bars were sprayed with automotive paint for color and rust protection. For additional ideas on decorating with plumbing pipes, see *Functional Sophistication, pages 84–89.*

baths

look when paired with vivid colors and fabrics.

1 Ceiling-Mount Panels

The panels framing the bathtub are made from four fabrics. The secret to mixing fabrics is using different-size prints.

- Sew simple, sheer panels like these and edge with a complementary fabric, or slice 18-inch-wide strips from a full-size shower curtain or drapery. Hem raw edges. Tack ties to the top.
- Screw eyebolts into the ceiling. (Plant hooks will also work.) Tie the fabric straps through the eyebolts.
- To attach a heavier curtain, drill pilot holes for plastic anchors, insert the plant hooks' screw shanks into the anchors, then screw the hooks into the ceiling.

2 Bordered Sheers

White sheers trimmed in a fruit-motif fabric coordinate with the ceiling-mount panels and are airy enough to lighten the heavy tile. Start with a sheer fabric. Cut fabric to desired length. Hem raw edges. Add a colorful border using leftover fabric from the ceiling-mount panels.

3 Quilted Bath Mat

Quilting adds pattern and interest to this bath mat.

- Determine the size of your bath mat. (The mat shown is 24×30 inches.) Add ½-inch seam allowances on all sides.
- Before cutting, determine the dimensions of the quilting grid and mark quilting lines on the decorator fabric. Cut the fabric to size for the top layer. Cut a middle layer of batting and bottom layer of muslin 1 inch larger than the top layer. Sandwich the batting between the wrong sides of the decorator fabric and muslin; batting and muslin will extend ½ inch beyond the decorator fabric on all

sides. Pin the layers, then machine-quilt on marked grid. Trim batting and muslin layers to the size of the decorator fabric.

- For cording, measure the mat's perimeter; add several inches for corners. Cut 4-inch bias-cut strips to equal this length, stitch into one long strip, and press open the seams. Center 1-inch cording on the strip's wrong side and fold fabric to enclose, matching the long edges. Machine-stitch with the zipper-foot attachment next to the cording. Pin cording on the right side of the decorator fabric along the mat's perimeter; match the raw edges. Sew using a ½-inch seam allowance. Press allowance to muslin; topstitch through all the layers.
- Place nonskid backing under the mat.

4 Framed Family Photos

Family photos bring warmth to your bathroom. For ideas on how to mat and frame your favorite photos, vintage postcards, and greeting cards, see *Greeting Card Art, page 102*.

5 Storage Containers

Galvanized metal locker-style containers, like the one shown, come in a variety of sizes and shapes. Their water-resistant quality makes them perfect for bathroom storage. They can be useful for holding extra towels, loofah sponges, shampoo bottles, and bath toys for small children. Similar containers are available at storage specialty and mass merchandise stores.

6 Painted Vanity

Berry red paint and new knobs make an old vanity look like new.

- Remove all the hardware and hinges. Fill any chips or gouges with wood putty. Allow to dry, then sand smooth.
- Brush on stain-blocking primer made for humid areas. Let it dry. (If you select dark or bright paint, have primer tinted the color of the base coat.)
- Apply paint in the desired color; choose a high-humidity formula that withstands bath moisture. Let dry, then apply a second coat if needed.
- When dry, reinstall knobs and hinges.

baths

Pattern Perfect

1 Shower Curtain

A floor-length shower curtain made of inexpensive beige terry cloth is tucked behind the ceiling soffit. To make, follow the instructions for the *Floral Shower Curtain, page 101*. To embellish like the curtain shown, sew a black and beige checkered border along the center opening and the hem of the curtain.

Attach the border with snaps to make it removable so the terry cloth can be machine-washed. Fabric-store trim edges the soffit; attach to the shower side of the overhang with hook-and-loop tape.

2 Diamond Wall Pattern

The neutral wall color is enhanced with a sophisticated diamond motif.

- Prime the walls and let dry according to the manufacturer's directions. Apply a base coat of paint to the walls. Let dry.
- Choose the scale and placement of the diamond pattern. Finding the points of the diamond is the key to laying out the diamond grid.
- Begin by measuring and marking pencil dots on the wall. Start at the corner where the walls meet the ceiling and

301 decorating projects & ideas

Neutral colors and a harlequin diamond pattern give this bath a light, airy appeal.

measure half the width of your diamond design. For example, if the full diamond width is 15 inches, the measurement across is 7½ inches. In this case, measure every 7½ inches across until you reach the end of the wall. Use your own measurements to best fit your space.

- After the horizontal measurements are in place, measure down half the height of your diamond. If your diamond is 18 inches in height, measure down 9 inches. From the 9-inch mark, measure down 18 inches, etc., until you reach the bottom of the wall.
- Return to the top of the wall and locate your first half-width mark. Measure down from there 18 inches using a level, and every 18 inches until you reach the bottom. Continue measuring down the wall in this manner. Remember that the first mark down will be 9 inches from every other mark at the top of the wall. And every other mark will be 18 inches. You'll see a pattern emerging. When you finish measuring and marking, diagonally connect the lines with a colored pencil and ruler, and draw your grid. Tape off the diamonds just outside the pencil lines.
- Put a light "X" on each diamond that you want to be painted in the second color of paint. Apply the second color of paint.
- After the paint has dried, use a light colored pencil and a coin and trace a circle at each intersection. Use a smaller brush and fill in the circle.

3 Multiple Point Valance

This black and white checkered valance complements the sheer stripe fabric.

- On tracing paper, draw a rectangle the width of the window and to your desired length. Add the returns to each side. Cut out the rectangle. Fold

rectangle in half lengthwise and open. Draw a "V" in the center and one (or more) on each side, stopping at the returns. Add a 2-inch border. Cut out the pattern, and check against the window.
- Draw around the pattern on the color block fabric. Draw a ½-inch seam allowance all around. Cut out the fabric and a matching lining.
- With right sides facing, and ½-inch seams, sew the lining to the face fabric, leaving an opening for turning. Clip corners, turn right side out, and press. Sew the opening closed. Embellish alternating points with black pom-poms.
- Attach one-half of the hook-and-loop fastening tape across the top of the valance. Attach the other half to the front of the mounting board. Mount the valance to the board.

4 Window Treatment

A mix of fabric, including a sheer stripe and black and beige check, brings pattern into the bath while allowing privacy.

- Select your fabric and cut to the width of your window. The window treatment shown is made of a sheer stripe fabric. For the length, allow extra material so the fabric falls to the floor.
- Staple the fabric to a 1×1 piece of lumber. Mount the wood inside the frame at the top of the window. Wrap two strips of wide ribbon vertically around the fabric and gather the bottom of the shade into attractive pleats. Hide the 1×1 with a fabric valance.

5 Paint a Vinyl Floor

A checkerboard pattern transforms a solid color floor.

- Glue down all loose areas of vinyl.

Clean the floor as usual; let dry.
- Sand lightly with sandpaper or a hand sander (depending on the square footage of the room) to rough up the surface so the primer and paint will adhere.
- Choose a primer (an alcohol-based primer was used on the floor shown). Have the store tint it to match the base paint color.
- Protect the surfaces you don't want to paint with drop cloths or tape. Pour primer into a paint tray, and dip a roller into it. Roll primer onto the floor, starting in a corner opposite the doorway. Let dry according to manufacturer's directions. **Note:** Primer will even out the floor's surface, even if the vinyl is lightly textured.
- Come up with a design for the floor. A square pattern in cream and taupe with black accent squares was used for the floor shown. Choose a latex or oil-base paint that will adhere to the primer. (Read the primer's label to be sure.) Using a roller, apply base color of paint to the entire floor and let dry per the label's instructions.
- Begin the design work by marking the design on the base coat with a yardstick and pencil; tape off the areas that will be a different color from the base coat.
- Use a brush (for an intricate design) or a roller (for large-scale work) to apply the contrasting paint color or design. Let dry. Remove the tape.
- Tape off other areas and repeat for other colors or design layers as necessary. Let paint dry at each step, then remove the tape.
- When the design is complete, roll on three or four coats of polyurethane. Allow time to dry between coats.

6   Painted Countertop

Hand-painted lettering adds an element of fun to this countertop.

- Glue down any portions of laminate that might have come loose from the substrate. Clean the surface as you normally would.
- Protect what you don't want to paint with tape or drop cloths.
- Choose a primer. An alcohol-base primer was used on the countertop shown. Ask someone at the paint store to tint it to the same color as the base paint. Brush or roll on the primer; let dry according to the manufacturer's directions.
- Draw your design on the countertop. (The countertop shown has a taupe square on either side of the sink.) Protect the areas you don't want to paint with quick-release tape, then roll or brush on the base coat of paint. Let dry according to the label's instructions.
- Tape off the areas of the design that will be a different color from your base

coat, then roll or brush on the second color of paint. Let paint dry. Remove the tape.

- For lettering, such as the "his" and "hers" labels on the counter shown, either stencil the letters onto the counter, or draw the words on black arts paper (available at arts supply stores) and cut out each letter with a crafts knife. Mount the letters onto the counter with spray adhesive. The latter option is best for a less-trafficked room, such as a guest bath.
- Protect your design with three or four coats of polyurethane, letting each coat dry thoroughly.

7   Paint a Vanity

The room's neutral color and diamond pattern was also picked up on the vanity. To paint, follow the project instructions for the *Painted Vanity, page 105*. To paint the diamond inside the cabinet door inlay, begin by outlining your diamond. Measure and mark the midpoint of the

diamond at the top and bottom portion of the inlay with a pencil. Measure the length between the two points to find the midpoint, and mark the horizontal points of the diamond. Diagonally connect the lines with a pencil and ruler. Tape off the diamond just outside the pencil lines. Apply paint in the desired color. Let dry.

8   Embellish a Towel

It's easy to add fine details to a plain terry cloth towel. Purchase inexpensive towels at a department store. (The towels shown are cream, black, and taupe.) Attach store-bought pom-pom trim and rickrack using snaps that are sewn to the trim and the towel. The snaps allow the trim to be removed and the towels machine-washed. Hook-and-loop tape will also work instead of snaps.

Finishing Touches

A stenciled wall and colorful fabrics are among the finishing touches in this bath.

1 Crown Molding

Add a finishing touch to crown molding by outlining with a paint pen. The crown molding shown is highlighted in silver. Pens are available at your local crafts supply store.

2 Framed Mirror

You don't need to settle for a store-bought framed mirror for your bath. The mirror that hangs over the pedestal sink shown started out as a simple vintage frame. First, find a frame in the size and shape you desire. Look for a standard size mirror to fit the frame, or have a mirror cut to size at your local hardware store. Cut a piece of foam core to the size of the mirror to use as backing. Attach the mirror to the frame using glazing points that are fastened every ½ inch, or take to a picture framer to be mounted. Be sure to hang the mirror firmly from a stud in the wall.

3 Create a Stencil

A shower curtain valance is the inspiration for this wall stencil.
- Prime the walls and cover with a quality oil-base white paint. (Look for paints that are formulated for high-moisture rooms.)
- Transfer the pattern from the fabric using a photocopier.
- Trace the pattern onto a sheet of clear stencil acetate (available at crafts supply stores) and cut it out using a crafts knife. Turn the pattern upside down and secure it to the wall above the plate rail with quick-release tape.
- Mix the paint in plastic trays to get the right colors, then practice stenciling on a piece of scrap paper.
- Use a small brush to paint the design onto the wall. To achieve a watercolor effect, don't paint perfectly straight lines. (**Note:** Check with the fabric manufacturer before copying a design for yourself.)

4 Fixed Roman Shade

This Roman shade is mounted halfway down the window to allow natural light into the room. To make, see the instructions for the *Basic Roman Shade, page 88*. Stitch a decorative contrasting trim to the fabric edges before you hang, as in the shade shown.

5 Marbled Cabinet

This cabinet is actually made out of wood and painted to resemble marble.
- Remove hardware.
- Paint with a semigloss background color. (White was used for the cabinet shown.)
- Use an artist's brush to randomly dab small spots of black and burnt umber onto the cabinet. Work in small sections of about 2 feet square.

- Dampen a 4-inch brush with water and in light sweeping motions, wipe across the paint spots to soften and blend against the background color. If the paint spots dry too fast, moisten with water using a fine-mist spray atomizer. Continue this process across the piece, working one area into another.
- Seal with a polyurethane finish. Let dry.
- Reinstall knobs and hinges.

6 Painted Mirror

This thrift shop mirror was given new life with two coats of gold metallic paint. First clean the surface thoroughly. Apply metal paint using a small brush the width of the mirror frame. Metal paint is available in a variety of colors at your local crafts supply store.

baths

Finishing Touches continued

7 Shower Curtain

These buttoned-down tabs do much more than secure this layered shower curtain to the rod. Once associated with country style, tabs now lend themselves to a variety of decorating styles. The piping around the tab coordinates with the blue in the valance. By layering the shower curtain, you have the opportunity to mix and match fabrics. To guarantee success in mixing patterns, remember the rule of three: Choose three scales—small, medium, and large.

8 Radiator Cover-Up

A wooden box with a metal-grille front conceals this bath's radiator and makes a perfect shelf for a potted plant.

• Measure the radiator. Allow a minimum of 2 inches' clearance at the sides and 4 inches at the top.
• Prime and paint 1× lumber for the sides, top, and face frame, inside and out, and let dry (there is no back to the cover). Cut the wood according to your radiator's size and the clearance space.
• If the floor is uneven, cut arched "feet" for the radiator to sit on, using a table saw or jigsaw.
• Once the lumber is cut, abut the top and sides and secure with wood glue and 6d finishing nails. Fasten the metal grille to the inside of the face frame with ½-inch screws. Place the cover over the radiator. **Note:** In case repairs are needed, it's best not to fasten the cover to the wall. If you prefer to attach it, use screws instead of nails, so they can be removed for easier access to the radiator.

9 Panel a Wall

Although it looks like paneling, the wall shown was actually finished with 1×3s and paint. There are two methods you can use to "panel" a wall. The first method takes the guesswork out of spacing the ribs along the wall, but locks you into a specific design. The second method allows more flexibility. Choose whichever method you prefer.

Method 1:
• Prime and paint all the wood and walls and let dry.
• Use a stud finder to locate your wall's studs (usually 2×4s) and cut the 1×3s to length. Check the 1×3 for plumb (true vertical) with a level, then drive 8d finishing nails through the 1×3 into the stud to secure the "ribs."

Method 2:
• Cut the 1×3s to size and secure them to the painted wall in the desired locations with construction adhesive. Prime and then paint the wood in the color of your choice. Be aware that the glue may tear the paper face off the drywall if you ever want to remove the "paneling."

baths

bed

301 decorating projects & ideas

rooms

Create a new look in your bedroom with styles ranging from modern to country to Victorian. Add a dramatic bed canopy wrapped in lavish fabric. Wake your room up with fun paint treatments on the walls, furniture, and fabric. Discover imported charm with fabric-lined walls and stenciled furniture. Create a teen retreat with flea market finds. Decorate a girl's room in a farm-fresh country style.

50 projects & ideas

Colorful Wake-Up Call   Fresh paint, fun wall

1 | Linen-Look Walls

The walls in this bedroom are "textured" with a linen-look paint treatment. If you paint the walls without a partner, use an oil-base paint, which doesn't dry as quickly as latex.

Materials
- Surfacing compound (optional)
- Two shades of latex paint in the same hue (colors shown are two lavenders that are three steps away from each other on a paint strip) in eggshell or semigloss finish
- Latex glazing medium

- Patch holes or cracks in the walls with a putty knife and surfacing compound. Let dry, then sand smooth. Protect molding and window and door casings with quick-release tape; place drop cloths on the floor. Open windows and turn on a fan for proper ventilation.
- Pour the darker shade of paint into a tray; dip a roller into it, blot off the excess, and roll paint onto the walls. Let it dry according to the manufacturer's instructions.

- Mix 3 parts latex glazing medium with 1 part lighter-color paint in a large bucket; stir. (The glaze will appear white, but it dries clear.) Pour some of the mixture into a paint tray.

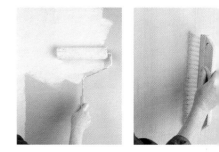

- Roll the glaze-paint mixture onto the wall in straight, 3-foot vertical strips from ceiling to floor, *opposite left*. Do not overlap the strips. After you've rolled three strips, have a helper slowly pull a dragging brush straight down the wall with a firm hand. After each drag, wipe the brush with a clean, lint-free cloth to remove the glaze. After strips have been vertically dragged, drag the same brush horizontally across the wall, keeping the brush level, *opposite right*. This creates a linenlike pattern. Wipe off brush after each drag.
- Continue across the wall, staggering the ends of the horizontal lines so there's no definite end marks. Let each wall dry completely before starting the next so you don't smudge a corner.

2 Detailed Dresser

An unfinished dresser was transformed using a notched squeegee and a paint-glaze mix.

Materials
- Unfinished dresser or other furniture
- Primer
- White enamel paint in semigloss finish
- Lavender (or desired color) enamel paint
- Latex glazing medium
- Polyurethane

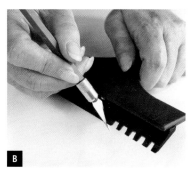

- Remove knobs or pulls. Apply primer to unfinished furniture according to the label's instructions; let dry thoroughly.
- Apply white enamel semigloss paint to the entire dresser; let dry.
- Tape off the edges of each drawer front, pressing firmly for a crisp edge, *Photo A*.
- If you're using a plain squeegee, mark the blade with a fine-tip marking pen every ¼ inch. Cut out every other notch with a crafts knife, *Photo B*.
- Mix lavender enamel paint and latex glazing medium in a 1-to-1 ratio in a bucket; stir. Pour some mixture into a paint tray. With a 3-inch roller, apply mixture to a drawer front, *Photo C*.
- Immediately pull the notched squeegee across the drawer front to

remove some of the glaze-paint mixture. Wipe the squeegee with a lint-free cloth, then drag the squeegee perpendicular to the first squeegee marks to make a gingham pattern, *Photo D*. Wipe the blade clean.
- Continue this process on the drawer fronts one at a time. Let dry.
- Paint the drawer knobs with undiluted lavender paint; allow to dry. Screw knobs to drawers.
- Apply polyurethane to entire dresser, letting it dry thoroughly between coats.

bedrooms

Colorful Wake-Up Call

3 Painted Curtains

A design from a flowerpot with a raised leaf-and-flower motif was enlarged and simplified to use as a stencil and stamp pattern for this window treatment.

Materials
- Fabric paint in desired colors (colors shown are two medium tones of blue that are beside each other on a paint strip, plus periwinkle and yellow-green)
- Purchased curtains

- Purchase curtains in a sheer white fabric. The curtains shown are floor length with ties at the top.
- To make a design-background stamp, place a sheet of white paper over the raised design of a flowerpot or other item, and rub the broad side of a pencil tip over it to transfer the image to the paper. Enlarge the pattern to the desired size on a photocopier. With a crafts knife, cut out the paper image, leaving ¼ inch all around, *Photo A*. (Do not cut out the details of the image.)
- Place paper pattern atop a flat kitchen sponge, and trace it with a pencil or fine-point marking pen. Cut out with

scissors, *Photo B*. Set aside.
- To make a stencil, repeat the first step with the desired image(s). Use a fine-point marking pen to trace the image from the paper to a sheet of clear acetate. Cut out the details of the design with a crafts knife, remembering that the cutout portions will transfer the paint. Set aside.
- To stamp fabric, protect work surface with waxed paper, and place the curtain fabric on top of the waxed paper, making sure the fabric is flat. Pour fabric paint onto a paper plate or paint tray. Dip shaped sponge into the paint, saturating the entire surface. Blot excess on a paper towel. Place firmly across the sponge's entire surface to imprint the image, *Photo C*. Continue sponging with various shapes until you reach your desired look. Let dry.
- To stencil the details onto the fabric, place the acetate stencil on top of the solid sponged background. Pour a different shade or color of paint onto another paper plate or paint tray. Roll a 3-inch roller in the paint, and blot to remove excess. Roll paint over the stencil to impart image details to fabric, *Photo D*. Let dry.
- Install rods. Hang the curtains.

C

D

4 Painted Pillow Shams

Painted floral pillow shams brighten up the lavender bedding. To paint the shams to coordinate with the bed skirt and curtains, see *Painted Curtains, Project 3*. Add a border to each sham by painting yellowish green stripes around the perimeter of the shams.

5 Painted Bed Skirt

Select a tailored bed skirt in the same white sheer fabric as the window treatments and paint with a leaf-and-flower motif to match. To paint, see *Painted Curtains, Project 3*.

Materials

- 4×5-foot preprimed canvas (available at art supply stores)
- Three colors of paint (colors shown are light blue, darker blue, and lavender)
- Flat-finish polyurethane

6 Painted Floorcloth

This inexpensive floorcloth brings pattern and color to a bare floor.

- Measure a 6-inch border all around the preprimed canvas; mark lightly with pencil. Center quick-release tape on the pencil mark, pressing firmly for a crisp edge.
- In center section of canvas, measure and mark alternating 5- and 3-inch stripes with pencil. Tape along each line, pressing tape firmly, *Photo A*.
- Pour one color paint into a paint tray. Dip a 3-inch roller into the paint and blot excess paint on the tray ramp. Roll the paint on the large stripes, *Photo B*; let dry. Rinse roller and let dry.
- Repeat above step with another color paint, applying it to the small stripes with roller; let dry. Rinse the roller and let dry.
- Carefully remove all the tape. Repeat step again with the third paint, applying it to the border with roller, *Photo C*; let dry.
- Using a pencil and a paper plate, trace a half-circle onto a scrap of cardboard for the border template. Cut the shape out with scissors.
- Starting in the center of each side of the canvas, trace the half-circle onto border with the pencil several times, stopping short of the corner. Draw the corner scallops freehand to connect adjoining sides. Cut the scalloped border with scissors, *Photo D*.
- With a paintbrush or large roller, apply two coats of flat-finish polyurethane to the entire canvas, letting it dry thoroughly between coats.

7 Scalloped Shelf

This pretty scalloped shelf requires a steady hand and good concentration when cutting the scallops.

- Use a measuring tape and pencil to draw a template for the scalloped apron on kraft paper. (Scallops shown are 5¼ inches wide by 4½ inches tall.) Cut out the template with scissors, then trace onto the 5×48-inch piece of

Materials

Note: One shelf requires a fraction of a 48x96-inch plywood sheet. To prevent waste, use scrap plywood you have on hand or save leftovers for another project.

From ½-inch plywood with one finished edge, use circular or table saw to cut:
- One 5x47-inch piece for ledge
- One 5x48-inch piece for scalloped apron
- Two 5x5-inch piece for ends

Additional materials:
- Wood glue
- 4d finishing nails
- Wood putty
- Primer
- Paint (white enamel was used here)

plywood with a pencil. Cut the scallops with a jigsaw or band saw.
- Repeat the prior steps for the two 5×5-inch ends.
- Mount the ledge piece ½ inch from the top of the apron. Secure with wood glue and 4d finishing nails, *Photo A, below top*.
- Secure ends to the scalloped apron and shelf with wood glue and 4d finishing nails, *Photo B, below bottom*.
- Fill nail holes with wood putty; let dry. Sand shelf smooth and wipe with a tack cloth. Apply primer with a paintbrush; let dry. Apply top coat of paint; let dry.

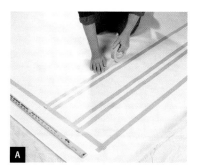

A

B

A

C

D

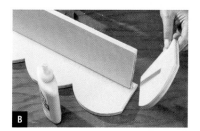

B

bedrooms

Import Appeal

Fabric-lined walls and a red-dyed

1 Copper-Tiled Bed

Copper-finish ceiling tiles give this bed a designer look. Purchase the ceiling tiles from your local home center. Cut them to size using tin snips. Attach to the raised bed panels with adhesive hook-and-loop tape.

2 Stenciled Bed Rails

The stenciling on the bed rails is an easy embellishment that delivers a stylish impact.

- Use spray stencil adhesive to adhere the stencil template to the surface you want to paint.
- Lightly dip a sea or cosmetic sponge into acrylic crafts paint in the color of your choice (red was used in this example), then dab paint onto the open areas of the stencil.
- Remove the stencil immediately, clean up paint smears, wipe the stencil clean, and repeat.

3 Refinished Dresser

This cast-off dresser was given a new look after the finish was stripped. Conventional paint strippers do the job, but they can smell like an industrial plant. To cut down on the fumes, use a citrus-based fragrance stripper.

- Wear old clothes and protect your work area with newspapers or drop cloths. Open windows for ventilation.
- With an old paintbrush, apply a thick layer of stripper, *Photo A, near right.* Leave on at least 15 minutes or as recommended by the manufacturer; if the stripper starts to dry, apply more.
- Gently scrape the paint off the surface with a putty knife, *Photo B, below*

301 decorating projects & ideas

elephant table give this room a far-off flair.

center. There may be more than one layer of paint. Use cotton swabs or old toothbrushes to remove paint from crevices, corners, and other hard-to-reach spots. Don't use metal brushes that can harm the wood. Reapply stripper to stubborn areas and scrape.

• Once you're down to dry, bare wood, use a sanding block to smooth the surface and remove traces of old paint and to prepare the piece for the new paint finish, *Photo C, below right*.

• Paint the piece in the color of your choice. Warm gold was used for the dresser shown.

• Liquid dye was used for the red accents on the front of the dresser. See *Dyed Elephant Table, Project 5*, for tips on working with liquid dye.

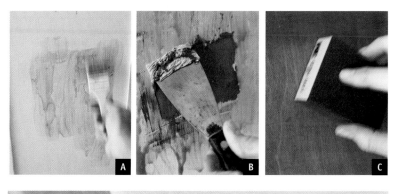

4 Designer Pillows

Pillows can easily be embellished with ribbon and felt flowers to give them a designer look. To embellish a pillow with ribbon, simply hand-sew ribbon around the edges. To add a felt design to a store-bought pillow, and see other similar projects using felt, see *House Dressing, pages 22–25*.

5 Dyed Elephant Table

This elephant table gives the room a far-away feel. The table has been dyed a jewel-rich red. Liquid dye used to achieve this look is available at discount stores. When working with liquid dye, remember to wear protective clothing. Mix dye colors for a custom combination, and apply to the piece with a sponge. Pieces like the elephant table shown are available at import stores.

6 Sheer-Paneled Walls

Fabric panels provide continuity and a dramatic look all around a room. To keep the look light, avoid heavy folds of fabric. To begin, sew enough widths of fabric, side by side, to cover the wall from picture-rail height. Sew braided trim on and loop every 10 inches. Hang the panels from decorative cabinet pulls mounted on the wall.

7 Desktop Decoupage

The top of this desk is decoupaged with paper sporting a Victorian floral design.

- Gather paper, scissors or a crafts knife, white crafts glue (such as Mod Podge by Plaid, which dries clear), foam brushes, a damp cloth, and a blank surface. You can buy special decoupage paper or you can find your own in books, magazines, letters, pictures, and fabrics.
- Before cutting, brush a thin layer of glue over both sides of the paper. Let the paper dry thoroughly.
- Cut out the image with a crafts knife or scissors.
- Use a foam brush to apply a thick coat of glue to the surface you're decorating. Spread a little glue on the back side of the image, and stick it onto the surface. Smooth out air bubbles with your finger, rubbing the image gently. Be careful not to squeeze out all the glue; wipe off excess with a damp cloth or paper towel. Wipe up stubborn glue globs with a paper towel dampened with window cleaner.
- Make sure the edges are smooth by dipping your fingers in glue and running them along the edges of the images; let all images dry thoroughly.
- To stencil around the desktop as in the photo shown, see *Stenciled Bed Rails, Project 2*.

8 Stenciled Lamp Shade

The lamp shade is stenciled and embellished with beaded trim. To make, use the same stenciling technique that was used in *Stenciled Bed Rails, Project 2*. Glue beaded trim around the top and base of the lampshade to add extra sparkle.

Teen Retreat

Design a retreat for your son using

1 Molding Canopy

This fabric-and-molding canopy dresses up a plain, inexpensive bunk bed.

Materials

- Desired molding (2½-inch dentil molding was used for the project shown)
- 1½- or 2-inch finishing nails (for nailer)
- Pneumatic nailer
- 2d finishing nails
- Construction adhesive or hotmelt glue (optional)
- Wood putty
- Caulk
- Paint
- Fabric (yardage depends on height of ceiling and number of panels)
- Matching thread
- Staples

- Determine the placement of molding on the ceiling. Ideally, one length should be under a joist. Measure to determine the lengths of the molding, cut the pieces, and miter the ends that will meet. (Crosscut the ends that will abut the wall.)
- Locate joists with a stud finder; mark locations with a pencil. Use a pneumatic nailer and 1½- or 2-inch finishing nails to secure molding to the ceiling, spacing nails so they go into the joists. (You can also use construction adhesive or hotmelt glue to attach the molding; however, this can tear the drywall's paper face when you remove the molding.) Fill holes with putty, and apply caulk between molding and ceiling; let dry. Sand, wipe with tack cloth, and paint; let dry.
- Cut fabric panels to desired length plus ½ inch for bottom hem and 1 to 2 inches for attaching fabric to molding. Hem bottoms. Gather panels; staple tops to the back of the molding.

301 decorating projects & ideas

2 Closet Doors

The closet doors are coated with chalkboard paint and make a handy spot to write notes. First, prime the door or area you are planning to paint. Chalkboard paint is available in both an aerosol spray and quart liquid at paint stores and home centers. If you use the spray, apply at least three to five coats for a smooth, uniform finish. If you use the quart liquid, apply at least two coats. After painting, let dry three days before using.

3 Metal Chicken Feeder

A metal chicken feeder is the perfect width to hold rulers, erasers, and pushpins on the desktop.

4 Pallet Storage

Wooden pallets that once held plants at a nursery now store blankets at the foot of the bottom bunk bed.

5 Exterior Light Fixture

Look beyond the usual places to find what you need when shopping at your local home center. The fixture in the photo shown is actually an exterior light intended for porches and patios. The fixture provides just the right look when mounted over a flea market desk and bunk bed. Follow the manufacturer's directions to install.

6 Galvanized Bins

These galvanized metal bins, another flea market find, once held nails and screws in a hardware store. They are just the right size to hold games below the desk and create storage under the bed for sporting equipment and shoes.

bedrooms

Teen Retreat

7 Flea Market Desk

The top of this flea market desk isn't smooth enough to write on. To make the desktop useable, find an old school map and cut the wooden rod off at the top. Sandwich the map between the desk and a custom-cut sheet of glass.

8 Pencil Holders

Antique glass jars, once used for cream, canning, or store displays, hold pencils and pens on the desktop.

9 Homemade Corkboard

Corkboard, framed in home center molding, can be made to fit any space.

Materials
- 4d finishing nails
- Wood putty
- Paint or stain
- Corner rosettes (optional)
- 1-inch drywall screws
- One 4×8-foot sheet of ¼-inch plywood
- Crafts glue or rubber cement
- Molding (enough for the perimeter of the bulletin board)
- Roll of cork (available at crafts supply stores and home centers)

- Use a tape measure to determine the size of the bulletin board, allowing for the molding border. Pencil its placement on the wall. Use a circular or table saw to cut plywood to the size of the bulletin board; use scissors to cut a panel of cork to the same size as the plywood. Attach the cork to the plywood with crafts glue or rubber cement.
- Fasten the plywood and cork to the wall studs using an electric drill with a screwdriver tip and 1-inch drywall screws.
- Use a circular or table saw and cut the molding to length to border the bulletin board, mitering the ends, if desired. (For the bulletin board shown, mitering was not necessary. Instead corner rosettes join the horizontal and vertical pieces of molding.)
- Fasten molding to the wall with 4d finishing nails. Fill holes with putty, let dry, then sand smooth. Wipe with a tack cloth. Paint or stain, as desired.

10 Tin Novelty Buckets

These flea market tin novelty buckets have been painted and hung on the wall to hold magazines.
- To paint, first lightly sand, clean, and prime with latex primer recommended for metal. Allow to dry. Paint with a latex base coat. To simulate aging, rub a candle over the dry tray. Concentrate on the corners and the edges of the bucket.
- Paint a top coat with latex paint. Choose paint in complementary color combinations. Allow to dry. Place a drop cloth or newspapers under the tray to neatly catch sanded dust.
- Sand with a medium-grade sandpaper, which will allow the top coat to sand off wherever the wax was applied, exposing the base coat. Sand with a smooth, light motion so that the base layer is exposed under the top coat.
- To hang, locate a stud and nail securely into the wall.

11 Storage Baskets

Wire and cloth-lined wicker baskets subdivide large, open bookcases into more usable storage, perfect for CDs, magazines, and books.

4 Striped Walls

Painting stripes can be fast and easy if you use a roller.

- First, paint the entire room a base color using latex paint. Aqua was the base color for the room shown.
- Use a pencil to mark the top and bottom of the painted wall every 8 inches, then connect the marks with a yardstick.
- Paint the darker color of latex stripes with a 6½-inch-wide foam roller, pulling the roller down each 8-inch stripe twice. Let dry.

1 Headboard Coop

An old 60-inch-wide galvanized chicken coop makes a one-of-a-kind country-style headboard for this girl's room. It provides plenty of cubbies for books, toys, and flowers. The one shown was rescued from a farm and thoroughly cleaned for obvious hygienic reasons and to bring out the rustic patina. It sits inside a wooden base to keep it from moving around. The base has been distressed and aged for a country appearance. Look for old chicken coops at flea markets and farm auctions. You can buy a new coop at a retail store that sells farm supplies. The new ones come with a wooden mounting perch in the front that can be removed.

2 Vintage Cupboard

Wallpaper sheets add color to this vintage pine cupboard. Cut the wallpaper sheets to size. Slide the sheets under the cupboard's trim. Adhere with double-sided tape to keep the wallpaper in place. Because there is no permanent bond, you can change the wallpaper design as often as you like.

3 Metal Buckets

Galvanized buckets found at a flea market are nailed to the wall, providing a home for stuffed animals. For instructions on how to paint metal accessories, see *Tin Novelty Buckets, page 127.*

5 Table Coverings

Table coverings in cottage garden prints are layered on a child's table. Vintage coverings, like the ones shown, can be found at flea markets and antiques shops.

6 Painted Furniture

Child's chairs are hand-painted to coordinate with the fresh design of this room. For information on how to paint furniture, see *Cafe-Style Fun, pages 146–147.* To achieve this same look, imitate the color scheme shown here.

Unconventional Bedroom

Although the pieces in this bedroom are traditional in design, they are displayed in unexpected ways.

1 **Floor Touch-Up**

Color and character were established in this bedroom by painting a checkerboard design directly over the plywood floor.

• Start with a clean subfloor. Roll on latex primer; let dry. (If the seams between subfloor panels bother you, fill them with wood filler, let dry, and sand before applying primer. Be sure to

①

4 Decorative Branch

A tree branch can be used as a decorative element and is an inexpensive way to fill a gap. Simply clip a branch in the dimensions you desire. Prop it into an upright position using a bucket filled with sand. The sand will be heavy enough to keep the branch anchored in place.

5 Vintage Decorating

Collections of vintage pieces can add character to spaces that lack architectural interest. A barber pole, a dry sink, an old gate, and three firkins (old wooden containers) form an uncommon, but eye-pleasing grouping against a wall. A good rule of thumb when grouping pieces is to avoid selecting items that are on the same level. Instead, vary the heights of the items so the eye follows the pieces up and down.

vacuum and use a tack cloth to remove all residue before painting.)

- Roll on a base coat of latex paint. (The floor shown is a mustard shade.) Let dry.
- To create the squares, use a template in the size you desire. For the floor shown, a 12-inch tile that was left over from a bathroom makeover was used. Lay the tile on the floor, and pencil around it. Repeat the desired pattern across the room. Because this design should have a "looser" look, don't worry about perfection. Tape off squares using quick-release painter's tape.
- Dip a sea sponge lightly into another latex color. (Black was used here.) Dab excess paint off by blotting the sponge on paper. Paint one row, dabbing the sponge onto every other square.
- Paint every other row to ensure a spot to kneel and paint. Let the floor dry for eight hours before filling in the missing rows.
- Once dry, protect the floor with at least two thin coats of clear polyurethane. Let each coat dry before adding a subsequent coat.

2 Window Screen

Rather than hide the great outdoors behind a heavy window treatment, an English fire screen is propped up in the window. The screen allows natural light to show through the design and adds architectural interest to the window.

3 Window Frame

An old wooden window frame, found at a salvage yard or flea market, leans against the wall and allows the color of the wall paint to show through.

Finishing Tips

There's a debate among collectors on how to clean, protect, and care for painted pieces.

- To preserve the color, finish painted furniture with wax. Apply Briwax with a fine steel wool, and buff the wax for a smooth finish.
- For a drier look, wash the piece with Murphy's Oil Soap, and then use Formby's furniture polish. This will clean the surface without ruining the paint. Be sure to use a light hand.
- If you're a purist and are concerned about paint flaking off, use the piece for decoration only. Be aware that some peeling paint might contain lead, which is hazardous, particularly for children and pets.

Victorian Charm

1 Toile Paint Treatment

Black paint on white walls creates a floral pattern with Victorian overtones.

Materials

- Paint in flat finish
- Stencil-roller kit
- Paint tray (if not included in the kit)
- Drop cloth
- Quick-release tape

PAINTING TIP: Only flat paint is recommended for this technique, which includes the background color as well as the pattern color. Glossier paint is too slippery for the rubber stencil roller. If your wall is painted with anything but a flat-finish paint, repaint it and let it dry thoroughly.

- Position a drop cloth to protect the floor and surrounding woodwork from drips; hold in place with quick-release tape.

- Pour paint into the paint tray. Work the double-roller applicator back and forth so that the foam roller soaks up paint. If you can, first remove the rubber stencil roller, work the foam roller in the paint, then replace the rubber roller. Practice rolling the double roller on an old board or scrap drywall to get the feel of it and to get the paint flowing smoothly from foam roller to rubber roller.

- Roll the rubber stencil roller on the wall vertically or horizontally to apply the pattern; start at the top of the wall and work down. In the wall treatment shown, each column was slightly overlapped for a tighter pattern, but you can leave a space between columns for a different look.
- As you paint, hold the double roller at such an angle that the foam roller never touches the wall, *right*. Maintain firm pressure to prevent the rubber stencil roller from sliding down the wall and to achieve a consistent impression for each repeat. Do not back the roller up after you have painted a pattern; it's hard to match the pattern you already applied to the surface.
- Some double rollers like the one shown, *above*, have marks or numbers on a side that let you line up the pattern if you need to fill the roller with paint in midapplication. If yours does not, reapply fresh paint to the foam roller after you complete two applications of the pattern.
- Follow the directions that come with the stencil-roller kit to correctly repeat the pattern, or simply experiment. Some patterns look best when columns align; others are attractive when the pattern is stepped.
- When you finish, thoroughly wash the double-roller applicator with warm soapy water, let dry, and save it for another project.

2 Tied-On Panels

This window treatment, made out of striped ticking, coordinates with the black and white theme of the room.

- Measure the rod, and divide by 2. Multiply by 2½, and add 5 inches for side hems. This measurement is for one panel width. Measure the length from the rod to the floor. Add 4 inches for a 3½-inch hem and a ½-inch seam allowance at top. For ties, subtract the distance from the rod to the top of the window (about 6 inches for the panels shown).
- Determine the number of ties for each panel. Plan for one at each end, one in the center, and evenly space the remainder at 8- to 10-inch intervals.
- From the ticking, cut two panels. Also cut two 4-inch-wide strips the finished width of each panel plus 1 inch (for tie facings) and the determined number of 4×24-inch ties.
- For each panel, press under ½ inch, then 2 inches at each side. Machine-

stitch. Press under ½ inch, 3 inches at the bottom edge, and hem.
- Fold each tie in half lengthwise with right sides facing. Stitch together, leaving an opening for turning in the middle of the long edge. Clip corners, turn right side out, and press. Fold and press each tie in half crosswise.
- Press under ½ inch on short edges and one long edge of each facing.
- Pin the folded edge of each tie to the top raw edge of the panel. Baste in place. Matching raw edges, pin and then stitch the facing to the panel (with ties in between). Press the facing to the wrong side of the panel, and hand-sew in place.
- Tie panels to rod.

3 Vintage Hats

Vintage hats can become a decorative element by grouping them on a wall.

bedrooms

Victorian Charm *continued*

4 Tea Towel Charm

Old tea towels and a framed photograph draw attention to this bedroom window. Trim the towels with small swatches of antique lace and other fabrics. Vintage linens can be found at antiques shops and flea markets. Layer two or more towels over a curtain rod. Use the wire on the frame and safety pin it to the back layers of fabric to keep the composition from slipping off the rod. A vintage hat makes another attractive statement at the window when pinned to the layers of linen, *page 132*.

5 Embellish Bedding

Customize bedding by adding a row of antique black buttons.

6 Bed Pillows

Ready-made pillows can easily be personalized by sewing on a row of black antique buttons along the edge of the pillow or by adding a fabric flower in the center.

7 Bed Skirt

A strip of linen gives a black and white toile bed skirt a layered look. Simply finish off the edges of a 3-inch-wide band of linen or buy wide premade ribbon. Stitch

the bottom edge of the strip 1 inch from the bottom edge of the bed skirt all the way around. Stitch the top edge. Place in between the mattresses.

8 **Dressed Chandelier**

This chandelier was dressed up by draping black pearl beads and hanging

small black and white porcelain pieces. To securely fasten the porcelain pieces to the chandelier, start with small strips of heavy wire. Hook the wire through the handles of the porcelain pieces and twist around a sturdy section of the chandelier.

9 **Reproduction Art**

The painting shown is a reproduction of an older work. Similar reproductions can be found in major art museum shops. Many museums also have online stores. You will be more likely to find primitive American art in an eastern United States art or crafts museum.

bedrooms

Canopy Charisma

1 Easy Canopy

This dramatic bed canopy is not only inexpensive, but it's quick to build.

Materials

- Three 1×2s, 8 feet long
- Eight 1½-inch wood screws
- Primer
- 1 quart paint in desired color (off-white was used for the bed shown)
- Four plant hooks with toggle bolts
- Fabric straps (see *Project 2, Simple Canopy Panels*)

TIP: This canopy design adapts to a slanted ceiling. Simply adjust the length of the straps to bring the canopy to level. You can also size the canopy to fit a larger bed. The one shown fits above a full-size bed. For a queen- or king-size bed, add hooks and straps to support the larger frame.

- Measure the width and length of your bed and add a few inches to each dimension so the frame allows curtains to hang slightly beyond the bed perimeter.
- Cut 1×2s to length with a handsaw or circular saw. Abut ends of 1×2s and screw together to form a rectangular frame.
- Prime and paint the frame; let dry.
- Screw a plant hook above each corner of the bed to align with frame corners. Suspend frame from hooks using fabric straps.

2 Simple Canopy Panels

Rather than fuss about hanging the canopy panels at the right height, let the bottoms of the fabric panels puddle on the floor for a relaxed look.

Materials
- Four twin-size sheets (one for each corner)
- Matching thread
- 3 yards of fabric for edging, ties, and straps
- One full-size sheet for behind the bed (you'll need an additional full-size sheet for a queen- or king-size bed.

- Cut enough 6-inch-wide strips of fabric to border both long edges on two twin-size sheets and one long edge on the remaining twin-size sheets. (The full-size sheet won't need strips.) Press the strips in half lengthwise, wrong sides together; unfold. Align one long raw edge of the strip along a long edge of a sheet, with right side of strip facing sheet. Stitch the strip to the sheet. Press remaining raw edge of strip under ¼ inch. Refold the strip along pressed center; slip-stitch pressed edge to edge of the sheet. Repeat for the other sheets.
- To make ties, cut 3-inch-wide fabric strips 12 inches long. Press under raw edges of each strip ¼ inch; press each strip in half lengthwise, with wrong sides together; topstitch closed. Stitch the center of each tie to top edge of a sheet, spacing strips 4 to 5 inches apart.
- To make straps to hang the frame, determine how far the frame should hang below the ceiling (12 to 14 inches is good), considering sheet length. Multiply the desired distance by 2, and cut four 6-inch-wide fabric strips to length. Press under the raw edges of each strip ¼ inch; press each strip in half lengthwise, with wrong sides together; topstitch closed. Sew buttonhole at each end of each strip.
- Suspend the frame at each corner with a strap, slipping the buttonholes over the hooks. Attach the panels with ties.

3 Stenciled Walls

Aged walls and a fleurs-de-lis design lightly stenciled in bronze paint set this room aglow.

Materials
- Paint in two shades of mustard yellow
- Bronze crafts paint
- Water
- Antiquing gel
- Stencil in fleur-de-lis or other design
- Stencil brush
- Sea sponge

- Apply the base coat of the lighter shade of mustard-color paint with a roller; let dry.
- Very lightly apply the stencil pattern with bronze paint and a stencil brush at random points across the wall; let dry.
- Mix a few cups of darker mustard-color paint with 1 or 2 tablespoons water and 1 or 2 teaspoons antiquing gel in a paint tray to make a wash. Use a sea sponge to drag the wash down the surface of the wall, allowing the stenciled designs to show through. The lighter shade of mustard should also show through in random spots. Let dry.

4 Hand-Painted Dresser

Hand-painted swirls, lines, and dots give this dresser a distinctive look.

Materials
- An old dresser
- 1 quart off-white paint
- Acrylic crafts paint in sienna and sage green
- Antiquing gel or dark stain

- Brush on one or two base coats of off-white paint; let dry after each coat.
- Apply swirls, dots, and lines, as desired, using artist's brushes and the sienna and sage-green paints. Thin paints with water, as desired, for a washed look. To make dots, dip a stencil brush in paint and dab onto the dresser surface. Don't worry about keeping lines straight—the less perfect the results, the better. If you prefer a more orderly look, use stencils.
- Once the decorative paint dries, "age" the dresser by using a rag to rub antiquing gel or dark stain on the surface. While still wet, wipe off the gel or stain so only the corners and creases of the dresser retain the dark color. Let dry.

bedrooms

out

301 decorating projects & ideas

door
living

These projects make the fresh air even more inviting. Entertain outdoors with a hand-painted cafe-style table and chairs, or opt for a cozier party with a hanging chandelier and candelabra. Add a painted floorcloth or stenciled rug. Make colorful mosaic accessories. Uncover innovative containers to display blooms. Refresh tired window boxes. Screen your porch. Relax on a movable bed.

67 projects & ideas

Fresh-Air Porch
Fun fabrics and comfortable

1 Fiberglass Screening

This screen is made from fiberglass that will allow gentle breezes in.
- Purchase fiberglass screening at hardware stores. Buy the widest kind available. Cut it to the desired length.
- Cut strips of outdoor fabric for borders, and fold in half lengthwise (the strips shown are 11 inches wide for 5-inch borders plus seams). Fold under long edges ½ inch.

- Make a frame with strips, mitering corners, see *Easy Miters, opposite*; pin border frame in place to encase screen edges. Topstitch through all the layers of fabric and screening.
- To hang the panels, apply 1-inch grommets in the top corners of the panels, *top right*. Screw matching hooks into the porch overhang. Pulleys on the outer hooks help raise or lower the panels, *bottom right*. Add grommets one-third of the way down on the inner

edge of each panel for the tieback—the nylon line that runs through the pulley in the top outer corner.

301 decorating projects & ideas

2 Potting Bench

A ready-to-assemble workbench becomes a pretty potting bench using outdoor fabric to make a skirt.

- Purchase a workbench from your local home center. Apply two coats of exterior latex paint and let dry.
- To make the skirt, measure the perimeter of the bench, adding 20 to 30 inches for each box pleat; measure the bench's height; add 6 inches for the hem. Cut the fabric to these measurements.
- Pin a box pleat where the skirt will hit each corner of the bench. Cut a 5-inch-wide fabric band for the top; press in half lengthwise. Press under both long edges ½ inch; pin the band to the skirt top, encasing the skirt top in the folded band. Topstitch along the bottom band.
- Fold under raw side edges of the skirt ½ inch twice; hem. Press the bottom of the skirt under 3 inches twice; hem.
- To attach the skirt to the bench, attach the male end of nickel-plated snaps (available at marine-supply stores) along the top edge of bench, 12 to 15 inches apart. Apply female end along skirt band at matching intervals. Fabric tabs with snaps hold the skirt closed.

3 Cushions

To keep outdoor cushions in tip-top shape, look for padding that absorbs little water, such as Hollofil. Cover the padding with mildew-resistant fabric sewn with nylon thread. Use nylon noncorrosive zippers. Store cushions in a dry, protected area.

4 Fun Floorcloth

This weather-resistant floorcloth uses the same outdoor fabric as the screen panels.

- Determine the desired size of the body piece, adding 1 inch in length and width for seams. Determine the finished width of the border, double it, and add ½-inch seam allowances; border's length is body piece's length plus double the finished border's width.
- Cut the border strips and body. Press the long, raw edges of the border strips under ½-inch. Fold the border strips in half lengthwise, wrong sides together. Pin to an adjoining border piece; miter the corners, see *Easy Miters, below.* Repeat until border frame is complete.
- Sandwich the body fabric between layers of the border fabric, like a picture in a frame. Topstitch to secure the body to the border.

5 Scalloped Tablecloth

A tablecloth cut from yellow gingham oilcloth dresses up a small table. Create a scalloped pattern by tracing around the edge of a drinking glass and cutting along the line. Oilcloth requires no hemming.

Easy Miters

For a mitered border on curtains or pillows, follow these steps:

- For a 3-inch-deep mitered border, cut four 7-inch-wide fabric strips, two to the same length as the main fabric plus 7 inches and two to the width of the fabric plus 7 inches.
- Fold each strip in half lengthwise with wrong sides together, and press with a clothes iron. Open each strip, and place right side down on a large work surface. At one strip's end, fold both corners toward the pressed line to create a point; press. Repeat at the opposite end. Trim the fabric strip ½-inch from the angled folds, creating a point at each end. Fold and cut other strips.
- With right sides together, align one end of a long strip with one end of a short strip; pin. Stitch the triangular points together using a ½-inch seam allowance and sewing on the fold. Use the same technique to add the remaining strips to the border.
- Turn right side out, and press at fold lines. Along all raw edges, turn ½ inch toward the inside of the border, and press. Position the main fabric between the layers of the border. Topstitch through all layers.

outdoor living

Perfect Patio

1 Faux-Stone Patio

Quick-release tape and paint creates the effect of grout lines between the faux patio "stones."

Materials and Tools

- Concrete etcher
- Acrylic-base concrete stain in desired colors (For the patio shown, light taupe was used for the base, medium gray for the blocks, dark brown and black for adding depth, and ivory or buff for highlights.)
- Slip-resistant additive (available at paint retailers)

- Wear safety goggles and rubber gloves. Remove dirt and loose concrete using a wire brush or a masonry chisel and hammer.
- Power-wash entire slab with pressure washer or a garden hose fitted with a high-pressure nozzle.
- Follow the manufacturer's directions and wash the patio with a concrete etcher to rough the surface so the stain adheres. Rinse thoroughly and let the concrete dry for 72 hours.
- Ask your paint store clerk to mix slip-resistant additive into the base color. Use a long-handle roller to apply the base coat (grout color) of stain.
- Apply in small areas and work the stain into the concrete surface from two directions. Base-coat the entire slab. Let it dry for at least 24 hours.
- Measure and tape off a 6-inch-wide course of "blocks" along the outer edge of the slab. Measure off 8-inch intervals and apply tape the length of the slab. Tape off individual rows of "blocks" according to the pattern. (The patio shown uses 16-inch-long blocks in a running bond, but any pattern is possible.)
- Use the same technique as for the base coat and roll the block-color stain over the slab. Let dry for 24 hours, then remove tape.
- Use a small paintbrush or rag to lightly dab water-thinned stain on the bricks. Use contrasting darker-colored (black or dark brown) and lighter-colored (ivory or buff) stains for a textured effect and to soften the grout lines. Use a small artist's brush or feather to add veining.

This remodel includes a faux-stone concrete stain patio and a low-maintenance pergola.

Materials and Tools

NOTE: The pergola shown was built with foam-filled aluminum framing. Though higher in cost, it is lighter and easier to handle, and has a longer life than wood. The finish is powder-coated for easy care. You can also use cedar, redwood, or pressure-treated lumber, but apply the finish before final assembly. The lengths of all components will depend on your site.

- Two 4×4s for support posts (A)
- One 4×8 for header (B)
- Four 2×6s for post fasciae (C)
- Six 2×6s for roof rafters (D)
- Fourteen 2×2s for roof slats (E)
- Six galvanized joist hangers (or aluminum receiver channel)
- 3-inch deck or sheet metal screws
- Two post anchor brackets
- Masonry fasteners

Patio Pergola

This pergola is made from aluminum that promises strength and easy upkeep.

- Use a stud finder and pencil and locate and mark the location of the wall studs where the pergola will meet the house. Mark the location of the outermost studs on the concrete slab, then position the post anchor brackets in relation to the studs. Attach the brackets to the concrete using masonry fasteners. With a circular saw or miter saw, cut the 4×4 support posts (A) to desired length and install them in the brackets, using 2×4 temporary braces to hold them plumb.
- Measure the distance between the posts (outside to outside) near the top end and add sufficient length for the 4×8 header (B) to overhang at both ends as shown in the illustration, *right*. Cut the header to length, and lift it into place on top of the support posts (A).
- Measure from the bottom of a support post to the top of the header, and cut the post fasciae (C) to length accordingly. Fasten the fascia pieces to the posts and the header with 3-inch deck or sheet metal screws.
- With a level, combination square, and pencil, mark a level line on the side of the house the same height as the top of the header (B). Using the stud

locations marked earlier, fasten joist hangers in place with 3-inch deck or sheet metal screws so the lower edge of each rafter meets the level line.

- Temporarily install the 2×6 rafters (D) in the hangers and square to the header. Carefully mark the outmost

rafters to length, then snap a chalk line between those points to mark the remaining rafters to length. Label or number the rafters, cut them to length, then screw them in place at the hangers and to the header.

- Cut 2×2 roof slats (E) to length and mount the first one parallel to and 2½ inches from the side of the house with 3-inch screws. Using 2½-inch-wide spacers, install the remaining roof slats parallel to the first one.

Bug-Stamped Rug

This cloth-bordered jute rug is stamped with fanciful insects. Purchase a rubber stamp and stain from a crafts supply store. Randomly stamp bugs on the rug. Fill in using a small paint brush if necessary. Let dry.

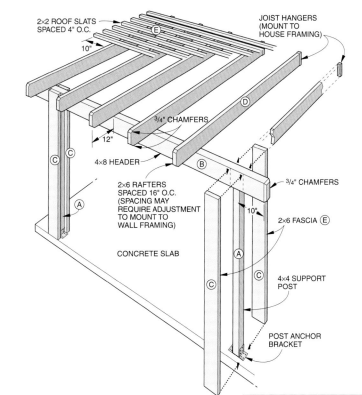

2×2 ROOF SLATS SPACED 4" O.C.
10"
12"
4×8 HEADER
2×6 RAFTERS SPACED 16" O.C. (SPACING MAY REQUIRE ADJUSTMENT TO MOUNT TO WALL FRAMING)
CONCRETE SLAB
3/4" CHAMFERS
JOIST HANGERS (MOUNT TO HOUSE FRAMING)
3/4" CHAMFERS
10"
2×6 FASCIA (E)
4×4 SUPPORT POST
POST ANCHOR BRACKET

outdoor living

Room for Comfort **Kick back and relax in this**

1 Bed Canopy

A garden trellis about the same length as the bed is the basis for this canopy.

- Purchase a trellis from your local garden center. Place the trellis on the floor and lay sheer fabric over it. (The canopy shown uses 7 yards of unhemmed sheer cotton batiste and drapes it an equal distance off the ends of the trellis. For the canopy width, 8 inches of fabric hangs over the front of the trellis and 16 inches hangs over the back.)
- Determine how high to hang the canopy. (The canopy shown is hung so the front is about 7 inches higher than the back.) The length of the fishing line to support the trellis is the distance between the ceiling and the desired height of the canopy, plus several inches for tying knots. Cut two lengths of 30-pound fishing line for the front and two lengths of line for the back.
- With the fabric draped over the trellis, choose two crosspieces at each trellis end for attaching the fishing line. Use a large needle to poke an inconspicuous hole through the fabric on each side of a selected crosspiece. Feed the appropriate-length fishing line through one hole in the top of the fabric, around the underside of the crosspiece, and back up through the second hole in the fabric. Tie a knot in the fishing line to secure the fabric in place, leaving plenty of line to tie to eye screws in the ceiling. Repeat at the remaining three crosspieces.
- To hang the canopy, screw four eye screws into the ceiling; make the distance between the eye screws the same as the distance between the attached lengths of fishing line. Lock the bed casters in place, then have two helpers hoist the canopy above the bed while you stand on a ladder and knot the loose ends of the fishing lines around the matching eye screws on the ceiling. Adjust the canopy position as necessary, and secure at desired height.

Place eye screws 18 inches apart in the ceiling and porch railing; if you don't have a railing, use the window frame or go from the floor to the ceiling. Attach the ties to eye screws as shown, *left*, with waterproof side of curtain facing out.

3 Movable Bed

This twin-size mattress sits on a plywood platform with lockable casters for convenience.

- Use a table saw to cut a sheet of 3/4-inch plywood to 42×80 inches; hide the cut edges with 3/4-inch quarter-round molding attached with wood glue and finishing nails. Apply primer, and let dry. Paint with latex semigloss paint (the bed shown is painted white). Let dry.
- Bolt casters into the corners, approximately 2 inches from the edges, and in the center of the plywood to prevent sagging. Place a twin-size mattress on top, and layer on the sheets and pillows. (For the bed shown, the mix of layers includes gingham, plaid, and patchwork in reds, greens, and blues.)

4 Bedside Table

This bedside table is made from a tall garden center container that sits on a base with lockable casters so it can be easily moved from place to place.

- Purchase a container from your local garden center. The container shown is 24 inches tall with a flared top.
- Cut a square of 3/4-inch plywood about 2 inches wider than your container's largest diameter (the base of the container shown is 22 inches across). Attach 3/4-inch quarter-round trim with wood glue and finishing nails to hide the cut edges. Prime and paint in the desired color.
- When dry, bolt 4-inch casters approximately 2 inches from the corners. Place the container in the center of the base, apply clear silicone caulk around the container's rim, then crown with a ready-cut glass tabletop, available at home centers and discount stores.

2 Privacy Curtains

These curtains block sunlight but allow breezes to drift through the screens.

- Measure the length and width of your screens. Subtract 5 inches each from length and width to allow air to circulate. Cut one panel each from waterproof canvas and from a coordinating sheet to your measurements. For ties, use 24-inch lengths of ribbon as a no-sew option, or hem seam binding tape. Cut as many ties as needed.
- Lay the canvas panel face up on a flat surface. Align the ribbon lengths in pairs. Aligning one end of each ribbon pair with the raw edge, arrange ties evenly along the top fabric edge, about 18 inches apart; repeat along the bottom edge, placing bottom ties directly across from the top ties. Place coordinating sheet panel face down on top, sandwiching ties between fabric layers; pin.
- Sew panels together on all sides, using a 1/2-inch seam allowance and catching ends of ties in the seam; leave an opening for turning. Turn the curtain right side out; sew the opening closed.

Cafe-Style Fun

A plain table and three ordinary chairs are brought together in a cafe-style setting using paint and pattern in vibrant colors.

1 Round Cafe Table

This fun and funky cafe table is hand-painted in a colorful, geometric wheel design.

Materials
- Flat, interior latex paint: blue, yellow, orange, red, white, and black
- ½-inch artist's brush
- Polyurethane satin finish

- Start with a round cafe table. The table shown is constructed with an unfinished tabletop and an existing table base. Sand lightly and apply two coats of primer; let dry for 1 hour between coats.
- Compose a design on paper and transfer to the tabletop. Lightly draw the design on the tabletop with a lead pencil.
- Apply blue paint with a ½-inch artist's brush, using short, multidirectional strokes to create a mottled effect.
- Repeat with the yellow, orange, and red paints. Paint in the center with white paint. Let dry for 2 hours.
- Outline all the shapes with black paint, using a small artist's brush. Let dry 4 hours. Apply three coats of polyurethane, allowing each coat to dry for 2 hours.

2 Green Folding Chair

Two shades of green diamonds and a sun-and-moon face design liven up this wooden folding chair.

Materials
- Polyurethane satin finish
- Flat interior latex paint: medium green, bright green, orange, golden yellow, black, and white
- ½-inch artist's brush

- Lightly sand and stain the chair. Apply one coat of stain-blocking primer. Let dry 1 hour.
- With a pencil, lightly draw the design on the seat and back. Fill in with paint, using a ½-inch artist's brush and short, random strokes to create a mottled effect. Mix the two greens in small amounts to create color variations.
- Paint the sun and moon face. Let dry for 1 hour. Using a liner brush, paint the eyes and mouth of the sun and moon face.
- Paint the framework of the chairs black. Allow to dry.
- Apply three coats of polyurethane. Allow to dry completely between coats.

3 Red Folding Chair

Materials
- Flat, interior latex paint: red and ochre
- ½-inch artist's brush
- Satin-finish polyurethane

Thick, ocher-color swirls transform this plain folding chair into art.

- Lightly sand and stain the chair and apply one coat of stain-blocking primer. Let dry 1 hour.
- Paint the entire chair red. Let dry 2 hours.
- Draw the design with white chalk and fill in with primer. Let dry 1 hour.
- Fill in the design with ochre. Let dry 2 hours.
- Apply three coats of polyurethane. Let dry completely between coats.

4 Director's Chair

Materials
- Flat interior latex paint: gold and pale green
- ½-inch artist's brush

A gold and pale green trailing vine pops out against a dark-colored director's chair.

- Select a director's chair with a dark fabric seat and back. Remove the fabric from the chair and lay on a flat surface covered with a drop cloth.
- Use white chalk to sketch your design onto the fabric, or secure a stencil to the seat and back with spray adhesive. Fill in with two coats of gold and pale green paint using a ½-inch artist's brush. Let dry completely. (This design, unlike those on the wooden chairs, will fade and wear with use. Applying polyurethane will stiffen the fabric, so it isn't recommended.)

5 Painted Floorcloth

This floorcloth defines the setting with vibrant color block diamonds and the fluid movement of waves. For directions on how to paint a floorcloth similar to this one, see *Painted Floorcloth, page 45*.

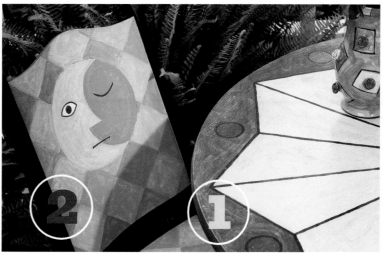

Captivating Porch

301 decorating projects & ideas

Dress up a potting bench for your porch and finish the space with a stained-glass window

An old potting bench can be given new life by adding some decorative touches.

1 Accessory Shelf

To add a shelf above the bench, screw a pair of scrap 2×4s perpendicular to the back of the tabletop and secure a piece of 1× lumber to the tops of the 2×4s with angle brackets and screws. Once the shelf is in place, give the entire piece a fresh coat of paint.

2 Decorative Brackets

Find inspiration for bracket designs from local architecture and books.
- Draw a design on paper. Transfer the design to scrap 1× pine, and drill a starter hole in the waste portion of the wood.
- Use a band saw or jigsaw to cut out the bracket shape.
- Finish by sanding the edges and flat surfaces of each bracket. Brush on a coat of primer. Let dry. Paint the brackets with white exterior latex paint.
- Attach the brackets using construction adhesive.

3 Lace Skirt

A lace curtain adds a soft touch to this potting bench. Measure the width of the bench. Purchase a curtain rod from your local home center and attach using the hardware provided. Thread a pair of store-bought lace panels onto the rods.

4 Mosaic Flower Pot

Recycle bits or pieces of a beloved plate, cup, or vase into a stylish mosaic pot.
- Break plates or fragments by covering with a cloth and hitting with a hammer. Wear protective eyewear. Use a tile nipper to cut pieces to size. Apply adhesive glue to the back of

each piece, press against the pot you are covering. Allow pot to dry overnight.
- Wipe off with a cloth. Apply premixed grout from your local home center to the entire surface. Make sure you completely fill between the shards of pottery for a unified look. If you prefer, you can leave the rim exposed for a decorative contrast.
- Use a tile float to smooth and even out the grout. Allow the pot to dry for several hours. A hazy film of dried grout will appear on the tile. Carefully wipe away the film with a damp sponge.
- Allow the pot to dry for a week. When you are sure the grout is completely dry, seal with a grout sealer.

5 Stained-Glass Window

This stained-glass look-alike will withstand the elements and provide lasting beauty.
- Purchase a frame from your local crafts supply store. Have a home center cut

a plexiglass panel to fit the frame. Clean the panel with warm, soapy water, and dry thoroughly.
- Draw a full-size pattern for your window design on kraft paper. Lay the pattern face up on your work surface, and position the panel on top. Press self-adhesive leading lines onto the panel surface, following the lines of the pattern below. Once you've positioned all the leading strips, apply a dot of liquid leading where lines intersect to imitate the look of soldered joints.
- Paint between the leading lines with acrylic glass stains. For a textured finish, apply stain with a flat feathering brush in overlapping comma-shape strokes. Increase color intensity by applying more coats. Use a ¼-inch foam-tipped applicator to apply oil-base silver gilding paint to leading lines. Clean up mistakes with mineral spirits or turpentine. Let dry.
- Use brads to anchor the painted panel within the frame. To hang the frame outside, suspend it from the porch framework using eyehooks and "S" connectors with lengths of chain.

Urns with a Twist

1 Place Markers

These grass place markers will make a sophisticated statement at your next dinner party.

- Fill each urn with potting soil to about ½ inch from the top to give the seeds enough growing room. Plant the seeds about two weeks prior to the time of your event to ensure plenty of growing time.
- Sprinkle seeds on the soil until they completely cover the top of the dirt. Press the seeds gently into the soil, or cover with a light layer of soil. Water thoroughly.
- Place urns in an east- or west-facing window (or any window with medium-bright light) or under an indoor grow light. Use a spray bottle to water the urns every other day so the soil stays moist. Seeds will take about seven to 10 days to germinate.

Materials
- One 5-inch cast-iron urn per person (available at local garden centers)
- Potting soil
- Grass seed, any variety (1 cup of seed is enough for six place settings)
- Water
- Copper plant markers

A

- To make the place cards, write each person's name on a copper plant marker using a medium-tip permanent marking pen. Gently push each marker into a grass-filled urn, taking care not to smudge the name. (Use nail polish remover to erase the names if you make a mistake or want to reuse the place markers for another event.)

2 Moss Spheres

Group at least three of these stylish spheres together on a side or dining table

Materials (see *Photo A*)
- One 7-inch cast-iron urn
- Three or four plastic-foam spheres
- Glue sticks
- 1 package light reindeer moss
- 1 package dark reindeer moss
- Several pieces of sheet moss (available at crafts stores)
- Green food coloring

for a stylish impact.
- Use a hot-glue gun to apply glue to the back of a small piece of light reindeer moss, *Photo B*. The size of the piece depends on the sphere size; you want the result to be a patchwork of different-tone mosses. Because reindeer moss is pricier than sheet moss, use it sparingly. Press moss firmly onto the sphere, using a cotton cloth to protect your hands and arms from burns. Keep a bowl of ice water handy in case of any mishaps.
- Repeat the first step using a small piece of dark reindeer moss, then repeat the process with a larger piece

of sheet moss.
- Continue to apply alternating types of reindeer and sheet moss until the sphere is covered with an even patchwork. Trim loose pieces with scissors, *Photo C*.
- Repeat with other spheres; place an appropriate-size sphere gently on top of the urn. They should last about a month if you keep them out of direct sunlight and spritz them occasionally with a spray bottle that contains water and six drops of green food coloring.

B

C

Urns with a Twist continued

3 Birdseed Spheres

Treat backyard birds to a sphere rolled in peanut butter and their favorite birdseed.

Materials (see *photo left*)
- One 10-inch cast-iron urn
- One 8-inch cast-iron urn
- Plastic-foam spheres (6- and 8-inch spheres for urn toppers; 3- and 4-inch ones for smaller tabletop spheres)
- Two bags of birdseed (one each of black sunflower seeds and a birdseed mix)
- Creamy peanut butter

- Fill a rectangular pan, such as a jelly-roll pan or disposable plastic-foam tray, with enough seed to evenly cover the bottom.

- Place a plastic-foam sphere on a table covered with waxed paper (or another protected surface). Use a butter knife or frosting spatula to smoothly spread peanut butter onto the sphere until it's completely covered, *Photo A*. To easily turn as you spread, insert a chopstick or tree branch ½ inch into the sphere.
- When the sphere is covered in peanut butter, roll it in the seed-filled pan. Use your hands to press birdseed firmly into place, *Photo B*. Continue rolling until entire surface is covered.
- Repeat for other spheres. Place completed spheres on another tray lined with waxed paper. Place in refrigerator for six to eight hours or until set.
- Remove spheres from refrigerator; set larger ones on urns. Place the urns or the small spheres on an outdoor tabletop or in your garden. When you notice the sphere showing through the seed, add another layer of peanut butter and seed. **Note:** The plastic-foam spheres pose no danger to birds.

4 Family Photo Collage

Urns can dress up a sofa table, mantel, or dinner table using your favorite family photographs.

Materials (see *Photo A, bottom left*)
- One 7-inch cast-iron urn
- Ivy plant in a 3-inch pot
- One spool of 16-gauge wire (available at hardware stores, crafts stores, and home centers)
- Photographs

- Use a wire cutter to cut six pieces of wire in lengths from 12 to 16 inches.
- Grip the end of a wire with the wire cutters and curl the wire around the wire cutter three times to create a curlicue to hold a photo, see *Photo B, bottom right*.

- Use pliers to bend the straight end of the wire to double it for additional stability (otherwise the wire will fall over when inserted into the soil).
- Repeat the two previous steps for all the wires. Place the pot of ivy into the urn. Insert each wire into the soil and arrange the wires so the heights vary and wire pieces are fanned out. Insert a photo into each curlicue, and press wire together to firmly hold photo in place.

Tip: Add some extra sparkle during the holidays. Spray-paint the wire curlicues in gold or silver and use them to hold holiday cards or photos with a seasonal theme.

Retro Garden Party

This 1960s-inspired garden party features a color scheme of yellow, bright green, white – and lots of daisies.

301 decorating projects & ideas

A

B

3 Daisy Cloth

Dress your table with a gauze cloth dotted with stamped and hand-painted summer daisies.

- Cut a square of gauze to comfortably fit your table. Unravel about ½ inch on each edge and run a line of fray-stopping product to prevent further unraveling. Carefully draw and cut out a 3-inch-diameter daisy from standard rubber foam. Lay the fabric over the paper.
- Coat one side of the stamp with white fabric paint, see *below*. Carefully press the stamp down and lift up. Fill in with a small brush if needed. Repeat for each flower. Space evenly over the table overskirt for a happily random, cheerful look. Allow the painted daisies to dry completely.
- Use a small brush to paint the center of each daisy with yellow fabric paint, see *above*. If you prefer, stamp yellow daisies and fill in with white centers. You can also vary the sizes and colors of the stamps.

1 Straw Hat Party Favor

These wide-brimmed straw hats are decorations that double as party favors.

- Purchase plain, wide-brimmed straw hats at a discount store. With an artist's brush, hand-paint petals around the brim. If you are unsure about spacing, mark first so the petals are evenly spaced. Taper the ends.
- Paint the center of the flower yellow, *Photo A*. Let dry.
- Attach green organza or other sheer ribbon to the hat. Cut at least 60 inches, depending on the width of the chair, so you can tie a generous bow. Secure tightly enough so that the hat doesn't slip, *Photo B*.
- Tie hats to chairs.

2 Striped Flower Pot

A terra-cotta pot hand-painted with stripes makes the perfect centerpiece for a garden party.

- Start with a clean, dry, terra-cotta pot. Mark pencil points around the perimeter of the pot to use as a guide for the stripes.
- Hand-paint the stripes with acrylic paint, using the width of the brush for spacing. Allow some of the natural terra-cotta color to show through the paint. After you paint the first color, allow to dry completely before you paint the second color.
- Allow paint to dry completely. Finish your centerpiece by planting your favorite flower.

Refreshing Window Boxes

Materials

- Window box
- Copper sheeting
- Copper nails
- C-5 light fixture with electrical cord and clear bulb
- Staples
- Sand or soil
- Preserved evergreen shrubs of various sizes
- Foam sheets or blocks (optional)
- Copper-color spray paint
- Glue sticks
- Small wooden stars or other ornaments in wintry shapes
- Sheet moss

A

B

1

Try one of these innovative ideas to refresh window boxes during the offseason.

1 Copper Snowflake

A snowflake is embossed into a copper window box and illuminated at night.

- Measure the front panel and two side panels of your window box, adding 2 inches to the length of each side panel to allow room for the light fixture. Add another 1 to 2 inches to the top and bottom of each panel measurement for end caps, which will be folded over and nailed into the window box so there are no sharp metal edges. Ask a metal fabricator to make three copper sheeting panels (one for the front and one for each side) to fit your measurements.

- Use a photocopier to enlarge the snowflake pattern, *above right*, onto white paper to the desired size. Use a pencil to measure and mark on the pattern where the punch holes should be located. Attach the pattern to the front copper panel with masking tape and punch holes at each mark using a metal punch and mallet, *Photo A, opposite*. Punch nail holes into the corners of end caps, fold the tops and bottoms of the two side panels over the window box, and nail through the punched holes to secure.

- Place the light fixture so that it will be visible behind the punched design of the front cover, *Photo B, opposite*, and run the cord under the box to an electrical outlet. Carefully staple around the cord to hold it into place, but do not staple through the cord. Leave 2 inches of space between the window box and the front copper panel, fold the end caps over the box, and nail through the punched holes to secure.

- Spray-paint the wooden ornaments with copper-color paint and let dry. Hot-glue the ornaments to the preserved evergreen shrubs so they look like decorations.

- If the evergreens come in pots, simply arrange them in the empty window box, using foam sheets or blocks to prop them up. If not, fill the window box with sand or soil, then place the evergreens in the box as desired. Finish off with mounds of sheet moss around the evergreen shrubs.

2 Ice Wreaths

These ice wreaths are illuminated with pillar candles.

- Place a coffee can weighted with rocks in the center of a square metal baking pan, add an inch or so of distilled water, and partially freeze.

- Place small sprigs of greenery on top of the partially frozen water, then add more water and refreeze.

- Gently pop the wreath out of the pan (and remove the coffee can) by dipping the pan in warm water.

- Nestle the wreath into soil in your window box or brace it with blocks of ice. To illuminate, place a pillar candle behind it.

3 Fruity Garland

Use a needle and thread to string a simple garland of blueberries and kumquats to add a colorful accent to the front of a window box. Secure the garland using small nails.

Refreshing Window Boxes

4 Bird Branches

Bring texture and color to a window box using moss, magnolia leaves, and floral foam.

Materials

- Window box
- Preserved magnolia leaves (available at floral supply stores)
- Staples
- Dry floral foam to fill window box (available at floral and craft stores)
- Corded white holiday lights (strand should be long enough to span the inside perimeter of the window box)
- Glue sticks (optional)
- Moss (optional)

- With a staple gun, attach flawed magnolia leaves to the top edge of the window box so the box will be completely covered. Then staple a full column of whole leaves, *Photo A*, so the tips of the leaves come above the lip of the window box. Secure each leaf by stapling it twice at its bottom. Continue adding columns, working from top to bottom, right to left. Overlap each column so there are no empty spaces, and overlap each leaf in a column to cover up staples in the previous leaf. At the bottom, fold the last leaf of each column under, and staple to the bottom of box.

- Fill the window box to the top with dry floral foam. Poke bird branches into the foam, packing them close together. As you place branches into the foam, weave a strand of lights around the branch bases, *Photo B*. The magnolia leaves that poke above the top of the box should conceal the lights. Use pruning shears to trim all branches to the same height, cutting the branches about as tall as the window box to maintain a pleasing scale. If desired, hot-glue clumps of moss around the base of the branches for added texture and to help cover the light cord.

A

B

5. Colored Glass Bottles

Glass bottles nestled into sand add color to a window box all winter long. Choose containers in various sizes, shapes, and colors that complement each other. The containers shown are green and blue. To illuminate, place votive, pillar, and tapered candles in some bottles. An electrical glass insulator turned upside down makes a unique holder for a votive. Sprinkle glass chips or marbles to cover the exposed sand.

6. Frozen Luminaries

It's easy to turn distilled water, assorted greenery, and colorful fruit into ice luminaries.

- Start with two metal cans (one large and one small). Bend paddle wire around the smaller can to suspend it in the larger can. Fill the larger can about one-third full of water, and freeze. Insert greens and fruit into the large cylinder, add more water, and freeze again.
- Slip the luminary out of the container by dipping it into warm water. Place a votive or pillar candle in the inset, and set the luminary along a path or on your porch steps.

Using Candles Outdoors

When using lighted candles in outdoor displays, remember to keep an eye on the burning candles and extinguish them before you turn in for the night.

Outdoor Entertaining

Candles and roses combine to make the perfect setting for an outdoor dinner party or intimate dinner for two.

1 Candle Chandelier

Dine outdoors by candlelight with this chandelier dressed up with small roses.
- Shop for a candle chandelier at shops that sell garden ornaments.
- Dress up the chandelier using florist foam and small roses.
- To hang, measure the length of chain you need and have it cut to fit at a hardware store or home center. Attach it securely to the chandelier and loop it over a sturdy limb, *opposite left*. Enlist help to hold the chandelier as you pull down the chain. Hook the chain in place under the tree limb.
- Purchase quality, long-burning tapers, *opposite right*. Light the candles at nightfall.

2 Architectural Pieces

These pieces of architectural fragments make a nice table display when grouped with a colorful mosaic pot centerpiece. You can purchase architectural salvage at flea markets and salvage yards.

3 Candelabra

These candelabras, typical of ones that you would find at a wedding in a church, can be found at shops that sell antique ornaments.
- Cut roses and place in florist picks. Fill small terra-cotta pots with florist foam. Push in picks and cover with moss.
- Alternate the flower pots with clear glass candleholders and votive candles, *right*.
- Add pots of English ivy to twine through the candelabra.

4 Mosaic Centerpiece

This mosaic pot makes a great centerpiece combined with colorful flowers, ivy, and fruit, then placed on a pedestal cake stand. To make a pot similar to this one, see the instructions for the *Mosaic Flower Pot, page 149*.

5 Outdoor Dining Table

This table is simply made from a door found at a salvage yard secured onto a stable, metal base (also found at a salvage yard). The door is secured to the base using clips. Before you attach the clips, set a level on the tabletop and shim if necessary.

Back Porch Color

1 Stenciled Rug

Concrete stain provides durability for this stenciled rug of stars and rich, red roses.

- When staining concrete, it is important to first prepare the surface. Scrape the concrete and pressure-wash it. After this, acid-wash the surface with a commercial concrete etcher, following the manufacturer's instructions and safety precautions. Let the etched concrete dry for 72 hours.
- Purchase silicon acrylic concrete stain, which is available at most home

centers and paint stores. (Avoid regular floor paint that will eventually flake on moist concrete.) Seafoam green, light buff, brick red, and blue stains were used on the rug shown.

- Determine the "rug" placement and use quick-release tape to mark its perimeter. Measure in 6½ inches from the perimeter and tape off the rug's border. Use a roller to stain the rug's center seafoam green. While this is drying, roll light buff stain over the rest of the floor. Concrete stain needs to dry 24 hours between applications.

- While backgrounds dry, enlarge the stencil designs (rose and rose details and leaf and leaf details, *opposite*) to desired sizes on a photocopier. Trace designs onto stencil acetate with a felt-tip pen; cut out with a crafts knife.
- When stains are dry, remove tape. Tape off a 5-inch-wide border around the seafoam green center, and stain it blue. Once dry, remove tape. Repeat the process to add a thinner width of red stain to the outside of the "rug."
- Use light buff stain and randomly stencil stars over the rug's seafoam

green center. Use a spray stencil adhesive to keep designs in place while you work. Use the brick red stain and randomly stencil roses over the floor's light buff background. Let dry.

• Stencil leaves in groups of two or three around each rose. Let dry. Use an artist's brush to paint a wavy line of seafoam green stain in the rug's blue border; add light buff dots between the waves.

• Stencil the details in each rose using an artist's liner brush. To make the details look hand-painted, mix brick red with light buff in a 1-to-1 ratio in one tray. Use straight light buff in another tray. Dip your brush into the red mixture, then into the light colors, and stencil the rose details. For some strokes, alternate the colors. Remove the stencil and make freehand strokes next to the details and intermittently around roses' perimeters. Let dry.

2 Hand-Painted Pot

It's easy to add a bit of uniqueness and character to an ordinary terra-cotta pot. To paint, start with a clean, dry, terra-cotta pot. Select a brush the proper width and hand-paint squiggles and circles with white acrylic paint. Allow paint to dry completely. Finish by planting your favorite flower.

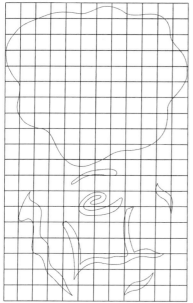

1 SQUARE = 1/2 INCH

1 SQUARE = 1/2 INCH

outdoor living

Back Porch Color

3 Mosaic Table

A combination of plate and tile pieces created a series of concentric circles to make this mosaic table. Each circle features a distinct color and pattern. Use tile nippers to cut pieces to fit into specific spaces. To make the tile tabletop, select a wood end table with a flat top. Put masking tape around the tabletop edge so the tape extends about ½ inch above the tabletop. (This allows you to build up a grout lip inside the tape.) Then, follow the instructions for the *Mosaic Tabletop, page 49,* for adhering tiles.

4 Stained Brick Path

This stained brick path blends well against the stained concrete rug because both areas use the same color of red.

- First prepare the concrete surface as described in the *Stenciled Rug, Project 1*. Purchase brick red and light buff silicon acrylic concrete stain; the concrete's original gray color will serve as the mortar between the faux bricks.
- Determine a brick pattern. Measure and mark off the pattern on the concrete with a pencil, delineating bricks and mortar.
- Cut a kitchen sponge down to brick size(s). Dip the sponge in the brick red stain, blotting off excess marks. Repeat until pattern is complete. Let the stain dry 24 hours.
- Lightly dip the brick-size sponge in light buff stain; blot off excess on a paper towel so barely any color remains on the sponge. Press sponge on all the bricks to add highlights. Let dry.

5 Chair Cushion

Wide ties and colorful piping accent this fun, blue and white striped chair cushion. For tips on the upkeep of outdoor cushions, see *Cushions, page 141*.

6 Fun Accent Pillow

This accent pillow is made from plain cotton fabric that was embellished with stamped flowers and outlined using a metallic pen. To make the pillow, cut two pieces of fabric to fit a pillow form. Purchase a flower stamp, fabric paint, and metallic pens in the colors of your choice from your local crafts supply store. Randomly stamp flowers onto the fabric. Allow time for paint to dry. Outline flowers using a metallic pen. To stitch, follow the instructions for the *Pillows, page 12*.

7 Mosaic Mirror

Antique doorknobs make handy hooks for this colorful mosaic mirror.

- Cut a 24-inch square of ½-inch-thick plywood, paint it white, and let it dry. Glue a 6-inch-square mirror to the plywood's center. Drill through the plywood under the mirror, and secure four antique doorknobs with screws and bolts.
- Follow the steps for adhering tiles that can be found in the *Mosaic Table, Project 3*. On the mirror frame, when positioning the tiles in mastic, first place the pieces along the frame's perimeter, remembering to face each tile's beveled edge out, then add them to the mirror's perimeter. Fill in the center, tiling around the doorknobs last.

outdoor living

Groundbreaking Containers

1 Earthy Container

Sheets of bark and moss give this container an earthy feel.

Materials

(**Note:** Quantities of materials should be adjusted to fit your project.)

- 1 metal or plastic bucket
- 1 sheet of ¼- or ½-inch plywood
- Wood preservative
- Wood glue
- Handful of ½-inch screws
- Paper-thin sheets of bark (available at crafts stores) or thin branches, cut into 4-inch lengths (for base)
- Nails
- 12×36-inch piece of chicken wire
- 1 sheet or bag of moss (available at garden centers)
- Cable staples
- Thin twigs about 32 inches long
- Twine
- 5 thick split branches about 11 inches long (for sides)

A

B

- Clean and dry the bucket if necessary. Use a nail set and hammer to punch holes into the base of the bucket for drainage, *Photo A*. Wear protective goggles and cut circles from plywood for the base using a jigsaw. The size and number of circles you cut depends

on the style of base you wish to create. (For the bucket shown, the largest circle is 1 inch larger in diameter than the bucket, and the small circles are half the diameter of the bucket.) Sand circles and brush with wood preservative. Stack the circles from

Create trendy containers using low-cost materials.

C

D

smallest on top to largest on the bottom to create the tiered base, *Photo B*. Glue pieces together. Drill or punch a hole into the plywood bucket base, then screw the bucket to the tiered base. (The tall base of the bucket shown is about 7 inches high.)

- Remove the bucket handle using a handsaw or wire cutters. Drill holes along the bucket top (you will later use these to attach the branch wreath to the top of the bucket). Decorate the shank of the base with thin strips of bark or twigs, gluing or nailing respectively.
- Lay out the chicken wire until flat. Apply moss with the smooth side facing down. Place the bucket on top of the moss, *Photo C*. Tuck the excess chicken wire around the top and bottom edges of the bucket. Secure chicken wire to bucket with cable staples.
- Create a wreath the size of the bucket top from thin twigs or another material. Wrap the bundled twigs with twine to keep them in place. Run twine through the holes at the top of the bucket to secure the wreath; tie ends of twine together to secure.
- Decorate the body of the bucket with the five thick branches evenly spaced around the bucket. Fasten them to the chicken wire and moss using three small screws inserted in each branch from the inside of the bucket, *Photo D*.

2 Stone Design

Use stones of all shapes, sizes, and colors to make this bucket unique and fun.

- Coat a bucket or planter with tile adhesive (a waterproof, cement like dry mortar available in crafts stores and home centers).
- After the first coat is dry, add a thick layer of adhesive where you want stones to be placed, working in a small area at a time. Press clean, dry stones into the adhesive in a random pattern. Clean extra adhesive from stones with a small spatula.
- Secure thick rope to the container top with more adhesive.

3 Colorful Stripes

You can easily make a colorful, striped container.

- Prime a plain container and let dry. Mark off stripes with a pencil.
- Paint the stripes by hand with a small brush.
- To preserve the freshly painted finish, seal with one or two coats of clear acrylic.

4 Branch Out

Sharpened branches transform an everyday bucket.

- Peel and sharpen one end of enough branches to cover the outside of your bucket. Drill a small hole 2½ inches from one end of each branch and string the branches together using thin wire. Wrap branches around the bucket with pointed ends up.
- Press moss into the wire. Secure the branches with screws from the inside of the bucket through some of the branches.

5 Funky Metal

Wood is spray-painted metallic silver to make this funky, metal-look container.

- Follow the instructions for the first step of *Earthy Container, Project 1* base.

- Coat the base with metallic spray paint to match the bucket. Attach to bucket using small nails.
- Cut a groove in each of two small wooden circles so they fit over the rim of the bucket, resembling lemon slices perched on the rim of a drinking glass. Spray circles with metallic paint and add decorative nails.
- Wrap bucket tightly with lengths of chain; secure with a twist of wire.
- Slip silver circles over bucket rim.

6 Pretty Mosaic

Find a new purpose for broken tiles and plates in this attractive mosaic pot.

- Cut pottery into evenly shaped pieces for the two top rows using nippers (be sure to protect your eyes with goggles).
- Attach top rows around rim with tile adhesive. Add patterned pieces to circle the middle of the pot, then fill out the rest of the container with random-shape pieces.
- Fill the cracks between pieces with adhesive. To finish, smooth the surface and remove extra adhesive from tiles with a damp sponge before the pot dries.

7 Slatted Bucket

Convert an everyday bucket to a handsome, natural-style container using nine wooden slats.

- Buy a container in any shape.
- Cut nine equal-size slats to fit around your container using waterproof plywood. (The container shown has 16-inch-long slats measuring 4½ inches at the top and 2½ inches at the bottom.) Sand the edges smooth.
- Drill holes at four evenly spaced intervals on the long edges of the slats.
- Paint or varnish slats as desired. Place around the bucket; tie with string through holes.

outdoor living

Perfectly Impractical Pots

1 Flower Cart

A flower cart sits near the front door of a cottage, filled with elephant's ear, baby's tears, potato vine, and petunias. The cart was built out of lumber and the bracket handles from old lamps. The antique wheel in the front of the cart was a flea market find.

2 Woven Basket

An herb garden is tucked inside a woven basket. The body of the basket is made out of green branches left over from pruned birch and crab apple trees. Yew branches form the upright supports. The handle is made from a grapevine. There is no bottom to the basket; it's simply soil. The basket rests in a larger flowerbed.

3 Sap Buckets

Three sap buckets filled with pink petunias are used as a window box. They are attached to the windowsill by driving nails through the holes originally meant to hold each bucket to a tree to collect sap.

Dirt Tofe

These containers offer affordable and innovative ideas for gardening.

4 Bicycle Basket

This wire basket, once used for toting supplies to school, now holds a terra-cotta pot packed with begonias. The bicycle, an inexpensive flea market find, is perfectly at home on a front porch surrounded by planted flowers and shrubs.

5 Three-Wheel Bicycle

This old three-wheel bicycle, used by a local business to make deliveries, had been stripped of all the working parts and was ready for the trash heap. The bicycle now adds a unique touch to a yard and holds a collection of potted petunias and white begonias.

6 Washbasin

An old white washbasin sits on a sunny ledge brimming with violets. The wide-open container makes planting and watering easy.

Creating Planters

To turn any container into a flower pot, drill a hole in its base for drainage. Or put down a layer of landscape rocks or gravel before adding soil.

7 Vintage Bench

An old bench from an antiques store sits comfortably on the front porch of this home. On the top shelf, three locker baskets, found at a local flea market, hold pots of begonias and geraniums. The bench is surrounded by a cluster of galvanized buckets and terra-cotta pots.

8 Concrete Blocks

These concrete blocks border a brick path and act as inexpensive edging. Typically filled with mortar, they now support succulents, zinnias, and herbs, including rosemary, thyme, and chamomile.

9 Flower Box

A blue-painted metal box, overflowing with a colorful array of plants, sits on an old wooden bench. The handles located on both ends of the box make it easy to transport from place to place.

outdoor living

Outdoor Swing

This relaxing garden swing

1 Swing Structure

You don't need a porch for this swing. It's freestanding and provides plenty of support for climbing vines.

- Use a paintbrush and paint or stain all wood members as desired, then let dry. Apply polyurethane or other varnish to protect the finish; let dry.

- Use a pencil and circular or table saw to mark and cut half-lap notches in the 4×4 posts (A) and top beams (B), the center in the top beams (B), and the notches in the ends of the cross beams (C). Drill counter-bores and pilot holes at the joint locations, then lag-screw and glue each swing frame assembly together.

Materials

The 4x4, 1x4, and 1x2 lumber may be pressure-treated pine, cedar, or redwood as desired.

- Paint or stain
- Exterior-grade polyurethane or other varnish
- Four 4×4s, 8 feet long, for posts (A)
- Four 4×4s, 36 inches long, for top beams (B) and cross beams (C)
- ¼×3-inch lag screws with washers
- Crushed rock (enough for 6 inches in the bottom of each posthole, plus more for leveling posts)
- Concrete mix for four footings
- One 4×4, 85 inches long, for swing beam (D)
- Four ⅜×3½-inch carriage bolts with nuts and washers
- Four 4×4s, 25½ inches long, for roof braces (E)
- Two 1×4s, 78 inches long, for roof beams (F)
- Four 1×2s, 56½ inches long, for lattice stringers (G)
- Twelve 1×2s, 32½ inches long, for lattice slats (H)
- 1¼-inch-long deck screws
- Exterior-grade wood glue
- Four ⅜×5-inch eyebolts

- Dig postholes approximately 30 inches deep, spacing as shown, see *Diagram B*. Pour 6 inches of crushed rock in each hole, see *Diagram A*. Set the frame-assembly posts in the holes, and brace them level and plumb with 1×4 temporary supports fastened to stakes in the ground. Lay a 2×4 atop the cross beams (C) and use a level to make sure the frame pieces are on the same elevation. (Add crushed rock to raise the low posts as necessary.) Once the frames are firmly braced, level, and plumb, mix concrete and pour into each hole to ground level. Let set two or three days before proceeding.
- Notch the ends of the 4×4 swing beam (D) with the saw.

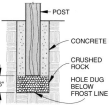

Diagram A

To prevent the beam ends from splitting, install ⅜-inch carriage bolts as shown in the detail illustration, *below right*. Fasten the swing beam to the frames with lag screws and glue.
- Miter one end of each roof brace (E) to 45 degrees. Mark and cut half-lap notches in the square ends, and drill counter-bores and pilot holes for the lag screws. Loosely screw each pair of braces together at a 90-degree angle, then lag-screw the mitered ends in position atop the swing frame assemblies. Tighten the lag screws where the roof braces meet, see inset photo, *opposite right*. Lag-screw roof beams (F) between the roof braces, angling them as shown.
- To make the lattice panels, place the stringers (G) about 9¹³⁄₁₆ inches apart on center on a flat surface. Use a carpenter's framing square to keep ends aligned. Fasten a slat (H) to each

end of the stringers with deck screws and glue, then every 9½ inches along the stringers' length. Position the panels on ends of swing frame assemblies and drive 1¼-inch deck screws through the slats to fasten the lattice to the posts.
- Drill pilot holes in the swing beam (D) to accept the eyebolts for the canvas swing, see *Canvas Swing, Project 2*. Also drill pilot holes in the roof braces (E) to accept the eyebolts for the striped canopy, see *Striped Canopy, Project 4*. Position the pilot holes so the eyebolts will suspend the roof's top tabs at the peak of the roof braces. Screw eyebolts into holes. Wait to drill pilot holes to suspend the canopy's bottom tabs until you've constructed the canopy.

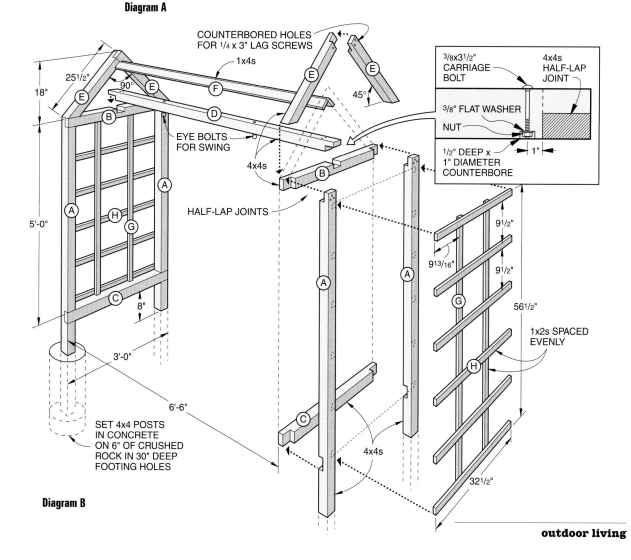

Diagram B

2 Canvas Swing

This swing is made of cotton canvas and plywood that's softened by a cushion.

- Start with the canvas fabric and measure one 27×90-inch rectangle for seat/sides, one 23×55-inch rectangle for the back, and one 9×51-inch strip for the front. On each 23-inch edge of back piece, press under ½ inch, then 2 inches. Sew ⅛ inch from the inner pressed edges. To make the back dowel pocket, press under 1 inch, then 4 inches on one 55-inch edge. Sew ⅛ inch from inner pressed edge and 2 inches from outer pressed fold.
- Press under ½ inch, then 2 inches on each 90-inch edge of the seat/sides piece. With wrong sides together, center the back piece on the seat/sides piece, tucking 1 inch of the raw back edge in the seat/sides hem as shown in Diagram A, *below*. Pin in place. Sew ⅛ inch from the inner pressed edge of the hem, catching the back piece in the stitching. Fold the back away from the

seat/sides and sew through all layers ¼ inch from the outer pressed edge of the hem. This second seam reinforces the back's connection to the seat.

- To make side dowel pockets, press under 1 inch, then 4 inches on each short edge of the seat/sides. Sew ⅛ inch from the inner pressed edge and 2 inches from the outer pressed fold. Close one end of each side dowel pocket by sewing ⅛ inch from the front edge of the pocket.
- Fold the front strip in half lengthwise with wrong sides together. Sew short edges together using a ½-inch seam allowance. Turn right side out; press seams open. Place the front on the seat with the open edge overlapping the seat ¾ inch. Sew through all layers ⅛ inch and ⅝ inch from the outer pressed edge of the seat hem. (Two seams add strength to the seat.)
- Referring to Diagram A, *left*, use a water-erasable fabric-marking pen to mark the position of the grommets. Be sure that the marks on the back piece align with the marks on the corresponding edges of the sides, and that the marks on the front align with the corresponding marks on the front edge of the sides. Insert the dowels into the side and back pockets before closing the pockets with grommets.

Materials

- 2¾ yards of 60-inch-wide canvas fabric
- ¾-inch dowel, 45 inches long
- Two 1-inch dowels, 19½ inches long
- Twenty-two ⁷⁄₁₆-inch metal grommets
- ¼ yard of 45-inch print fabric
- Extra-strong matching thread
- 50½×21½-inch piece of plywood
- Swing Cushion (see *Project 3*)
- Four 31-inch lengths of ⅛-inch steel cable
- 12 cable clamps
- Two 1½-inch (inside diameter) metal rings
- Two 20-inch lengths of ⅛-inch steel cable

Apply the grommets following manufacturer's instructions.

- For the ties, cut four 2×45-inch strips from the print fabric. Fold the strips in half lengthwise and press. Unfold strips and fold in the long edges to meet at the pressed center fold. Fold in half lengthwise and press again, enclosing the raw edges. Machine-stitch close to the open long edges. From the strips, cut two 18-inch-long ties for the front corners of the canvas swing and eight 5-inch-long ties for the back corners. Thread a tie through each corresponding pair of grommets; tie and knot the ends.
- Place the plywood on the seat and cushion, see *Swing Cushion, Project 3*, on the plywood. Thread a 31-inch length of steel cable through the back grommet on one side of the swing; loop through a clamp and squeeze with pliers to tighten. Thread another 31-inch cable through the front grommet on the same side of the swing; loop through a clamp and squeeze with pliers to tighten. Thread the unclamped ends of both cables through one 1½-inch metal ring; loop each cable through a clamp and squeeze with pliers to tighten. Repeat on the other side of the swing.
- Thread one 20-inch cable through each metal ring; loop the end through a clamp and tighten with pliers. Loop unclamped end through the eye of corresponding eyebolt screwed into the beam of the swing structure, then through a clamp; tighten with pliers.

22"

SIDES AND SEAT ARE ONE PIECE, 27×90"

SIDE DOWEL POCKET

SIDE

1" OF BACK IS TUCKED INTO HEM OF SEAT/SIDES

DOWEL POCKET

PRESSED HEM

GROMMETS

BACK

SEAT

FRONT 51" ¾" OVERLAP SIDE

SIDE DOWEL POCKET

Diagram A

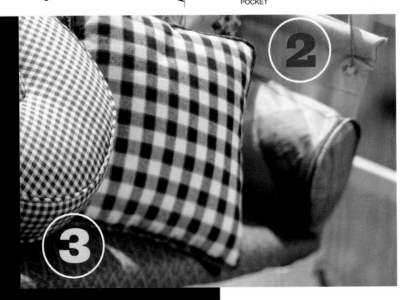

Fabric Tip

For best results, use waterproof outdoor fabrics, including awning fabric.

3 Swing Cushion

A cushion adds inviting color and comfort to the plywood seat of this swing.
Note: Sew with right sides together using ½-inch seam allowances.

Materials

- 2 yards of 54-inch-wide decorator fabric
- Matching thread
- Batting
- 22×51-inch piece of 3-inch foam
- Firm-hold upholstery spray-mount adhesive

- From fabric, measure and cut two 23×52-inch rectangles for the cushion top and bottom, two 4×23-inch boxing strips, and two 4×52-inch boxing strips. Cut a piece of batting large enough to wrap around foam. Use spray-mount adhesive to attach batting to foam; trim excess batting.
- Sew together the short ends of the boxing strips, alternating the 23-inch-long and 52-inch-long strips. Pin the assembled boxing strip to the cushion top, positioning the seams at the corners; sew strip to the top. Pin and sew the boxing strip to the cushion bottom in the same way, leaving one long edge open. Turn right side out and insert the batting-covered foam cushion. Hand-stitch opening closed.

4 Striped Canopy

This fabric roof keeps the harsh sun at bay so you can relax in the shade.
Note: Sew with right sides together using ½-inch seam allowances unless otherwise noted.

Materials

- 4½ yards of 36-inch-wide ticking
- Matching thread
- Three 76-inch lengths ⅛-inch steel cable
- Four ⅜×5-inch eyebolts
- Six cable clamps

- From the ticking, measure and cut three 52-inch-long pieces using entire width of fabric. Trim selvages.
- Pin, then sew the ticking pieces together along the 52-inch edges. To

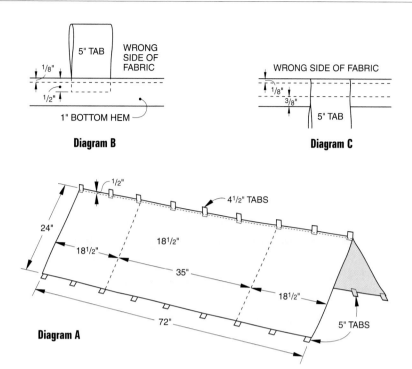

Diagram B

5" TAB · WRONG SIDE OF FABRIC · 1/8" · 1/2" · 1" BOTTOM HEM

Diagram C

WRONG SIDE OF FABRIC · 1/8" · 3/8" · 5" TAB

Diagram A

1/2" · 4½" TABS · 24" · 18½" · 18½" · 35" · 18½" · 72" · 5" TABS

clean-finish seam allowances, zigzag-stitch raw edges together, and press to one side. Trim the assembled canopy fabric, which measures 106 inches wide, to a width of 76 inches, removing equal amounts from each side edge. (Do not trim the 52-inch length.) Set aside the trimmed fabric for the tabs.

- To finish side edges, press under 1 inch twice on each 52-inch edge; sew ⅛ inch from inner pressed edges. Fold the canopy fabric in half, wrong sides together, aligning the raw edges; press along the fold for the top of the canopy. For the tabs, cut three 2½-×52-inch strips from the set-aside fabric. Zigzag-stitch one long edge of each strip. Press under ⅝ inch on each unfinished long edge and then ¾ inch on each zigzag-finished edge. Sew down the center of the strips through all layers. From the strips, cut nine 4½-inch-long tabs for the folded top edge and eighteen 5-inch long tabs for the bottom edges.
- Press under ½ inch on the short edges of the 4½-inch-long tabs, then press each tab in half. Referring to Diagram A, *above*, evenly space the tabs over the folded top edge of the canopy with 1 inch extending beyond the fold; pin in place. Sew ½ inch from the folded

edge of the canopy, catching the tabs securely in the stitching.

- For the bottom hems of canopy, press under 1 inch twice on each 72-inch edge. Press each 5-inch-long tab in half. Referring to Diagram B, *above*, evenly space nine tabs along each bottom hem, tucking ½ inch of the tab in the hem; pin in place. Sew ⅛ inch from inner pressed edge of hem, catching the tabs in the stitching. Press the tabs down over the hem and sew ⅜ inch from the outer pressed edge of the hem as shown in *Diagram C, above*.
- Thread 76-inch lengths of steel cable through the tabs at the top and bottom of the canopy. Loop each end of the top cable through the eye of the corresponding eyebolt in the swing roof braces (E) (see *Swing Structure, Project 1 Diagram B, page 173*), then through a clamp; tighten with pliers.
- With striped canopy in place, determine the placement of four additional eyebolts, which will suspend the bottom two steel cables of the canopy, in the top beams (B). Drill pilot holes, then screw in eyebolts. Loop ends of each bottom cable through the eye of the corresponding eyebolt, then through a clamp; tighten with pliers.

Index